Russell Allen Stultz has been involved in the electronic communications, computer, information and word processing, and educational and publishing industries for more than 23 years. He has written numerous manuals and books covering a wide range of electronic-technology topics. In recent years he has conducted international research, written, and lectured on management and productivity.

PRENTICE-HALL, INC., Englewood Cliffs, New Jersey 07632

RUSSELL ALLEN STULTZ

The Word Processing Handbook

Library of Congress Cataloging in Publication Data

Stultz, Russell Allen.
The word processing handbook.

(A Spectrum Book)
Includes index.
1. Word processing (Office practice)—Handbooks, manuals, etc. I. Title
HF5548.115.S78 651.7 81-10717
AACR2

ISBN 0-13-963454-1

ISBN 0-13-963447-9 {PBK.}

To my wife, Dianne, whose understanding, patience, encouragement, and constructive criticism provided the peace of mind and incentive essential to the completion of this project.

Interior design and editorial/production supervision
by Louise M. Marcewicz
Cover design by Honi Werner
Manufacturing buyer: Barbara A. Frick

10 9 8 7 6 5 4

Prentice-Hall International, Inc., *London*
Prentice-Hall of Australia Pty. Limited, *Sydney*
Prentice-Hall of Canada, Ltd., *Toronto*
Prentice-Hall of India Private Limited, *New Delhi*
Prentice-Hall of Japan, Inc., *Tokyo*
Prentice-Hall of Southeast Asia Pte. Ltd., *Singapore*
Whitehall Books Limited, *Wellington, New Zealand*

Contents

Illustrations

Tables

Preface

Business managers who are experienced users of word processing systems are almost without exception champions of office automation. They will tell you that survival without these marvelous machines would be difficult, if not impossible. Indeed, the machines *are* marvelous. They do things in a fraction of the time required when using manual methods.

When business managers decide it's time to automate their office, a casual look at the marketplace can be overwhelming. They discover that there are around a hundred different machines to choose from. Their dilemma: which one is best suited to the needs of my business? The answer to this question can be extremely complex. In fact, it often becomes so complex that many managers retain office automation consultants to help them in their search for the right system.

The consultant must first learn the business; the transactions, costs, functional relationships, common bottlenecks, and myriad business responsibilities and demands must be thoroughly understood before a system fit can be determined. Often, learning the business takes longer than learning about word processing systems. A business manager who develops an understanding of common word processing systems and applications is frequently better equipped to find a system fit than an outside consultant. Hence, *The Word Processing Handbook*.

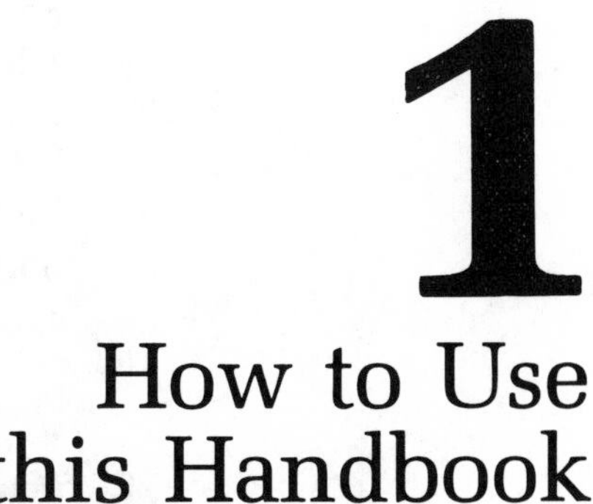

1 How to Use this Handbook

1-1. INTRODUCTION

Who this book is for

This handbook has been written primarily for the use of business managers who need to know about word processing systems. However, it has value for almost anyone in the information processing field, from keyboard operators who want to know more about the systems they use to computer system analysts who may want to integrate word processing features into their computer systems. Once you've learned your way around the book, it should serve as a valuable reference source. It provides, from front to back,

1. Some tips on how to use this book and a dictionary of terminology commonly used in the word processing field

2. Information about how office workers typically react when confronted with new technology equipment

3. A brief overview on the evolution of word processing equipment over the years and some insight into software, that all-too-often mysterious and intimidating medium

4. A description of how word processors can be applied to typical business problems

5. Information about the functional and physical structures of word processing equipment

Topics covered

6. An overview of input and output devices, methods, and media

7. A description of personal and centralized dictation equipment and how it can be integrated into a text-processing environment

8. An approach to analyzing specific business needs and identifying costly bottlenecks

9. Some ways to get the most out of your time when looking at candidate systems

10. A rational approach to financial justification.

1-2. HANDBOOK ORGANIZATION AND CONVENTIONS

Finding your way around

The book is organized into ten chapters, and each chapter is divided into numbered paragraphs. The chapters are numbered 1 through 10. Paragraph headings are numbered in sequence within each chapter. For example, the first paragraph number in Chapter 1 is paragraph 1-1; the second is 1-2. Major subjects within chapters are in bold type. The heading above, HANDBOOK ORGANIZATION AND CONVENTIONS, is a major subject. All the information that pertains to the major subject is contained in the paragraphs, illustrations, and tables which follow it.

Chapter numbers also precede figure and table numbers. For example, the first illustration in Chapter 2 is "Figure 2-1," and the second table in Chapter 3 is "Table 3-2." A table of contents, list of illustrations, and list of tables is included in the front of the book to help you look up information. An alphabetical index is located at the back of the book, containing subjects and page numbers. For example, if you wish to look up telecommunications, you'll find the alphabetical index refers you to several locations in the book.

How to locate information

When a figure or table is referred to in the text, you'll usually find it located on the same page or a facing page. Of course, this is not always possible, particularly when the figure or illustration occupies one or more pages. When this is the case, the figure or illustration will be located as close to the reference as possible.

Illustrations and tables

1-3. EXECUTIVE OVERVIEW STATEMENTS

Note that brief statements describing the contents of the book are located in the margin of each page. These statements are meant to help the busy business manager to survey material and quickly "zero in" on information of interest.

1-4. WORD PROCESSING SYSTEM TERMINOLOGY DEFINED

Some common terms

Before we start describing word processing systems, you should familiarize yourself with some basic terminology, or jargon, used in word processing. Some of the terminology used in word processing is also used in computer technology. This is because many modern word processors are actually computer systems. Instead of working on accounting problems, they work on manipulating fields of alphabetical and numerical characters. The terms and definitions are arranged in alphabetical order in Table 1-1. Where possible, technical terms are avoided in the definitions. Where technical terms are used, you'll find them defined in the table.

Table 1-1. Word Processing Terms and Definitions

Term	Definition
2270, 2741, 2780, 3780, etc.	Designations for communication codes (sometimes called protocols) used by data processing and word processing sytems.
Access	Obtaining control of a device, function, or system.
Acoustic Coupler	A device used to convert digital data signals to audio signals, or vice versa, and couple those signals between a data processing or word processing system and a telephone system.
Administrative Support System	A special word processing system with special features aimed at improving executive productivity.
Archiving	The process of storing data files on system-compatible media.
ASCII	American Standard Code for Information Interchange; a standard digital code used by computers to represent characters.
Asynchronous	Communicating with other devices without requiring a continuous exchange of synchronization signals.
Author (Dictation)	The person who originates and records words on a tape recorder.
Autoanswer, Autocall, Autodial	Automatic telecommunications features which preclude the need for manual answering, calling, or dialing during the performance of a telecommunication transaction.
Automatic	Any sequence of events performed automatically by a word processing system. For example, automatic centering relieves the operator from counting spaces manually in order to center text between page margins.
Autoscore	Automatic underlining of a field of text.
Background	The performance of a function, such as telecommunication, by a system which is transparent to the operator. While a background operation is being performed, the operator can perform another function actively displayed in foreground.
Backing In	Making a preconceived set of numbers appear rational.
Baud	A unit of measure used to describe data transmission speeds. Derived from the term Baudot Code after Emil

Table 1-1 (continued)

Term	Definition
	Baudot, inventor of the first constant length teleprinter code in 1874.
Bisynchronous	Continuously exchanging synchronization signals with other devices within a system to achieve communications.
Bit	A single data signal, either high or low ("one" or "zero"), used with other bits to form a code representing a character, number, or symbol definable by a digital computer.
Business Model	A mathematical model of a business designed to establish and analyze operational indices to determine business performance.
Byte	A series of bits representing a character, number, or symbol. A byte may consist of any number of bits.
Character String	Any unique set of characters and spaces.
Cluster	A group of terminals and other devices operating together to form a multiple-access system.
Code Key	A special instruction key on a data processing or word processing system keyboard.
Cost of Ownership	The total cost of system operation, including all expenditures for equipment, supplies, make-ready, service, training, space, etc.
CPU	Central Processing Unit; the portion of a computer system that controls data flow and executes instructions.
Crash	An expression used when a data processing or word processing system becomes inoperable.
Crossfoot	To add both numerical rows and columns (across and down) of a numerical table.
CRT	Cathode Ray Tube; the most common type of display.
Cue (or Queue)	In dictation, a signal used by an author to direct a transcriptionist to special information on a tape.
Cursor	A bright rectangle or underscore mark displayed on a screen to indicate the point of character entry on the screen.

Table 1-1 (continued)

Term	Definition
Daisy Printer	A relatively fast impact printer using a rotating type font resembling a disk with spokes (like daisy petals).
Data	Information in a form that is compatible for processing either manually or by a data processing or word processing system.
Data Set	A telephone instrument commonly used for data processing and word processing system communications in conjunction with a modem.
Decimal Tab	A special typing tab used to align decimal points within columns of numbers.
Default	A predetermined variable that is used by a data processing or word processing system when the system operator does not override the variable with keyboard entry. For example, a system may default to ten-pitch type unless the operator enters "8" or "12" in place of "10."
Disk or Diskette	A flat magnetic disk, resembling a phonograph record, used to store data.
Display	A TV-like screen or strip used to display information.
Distributed Logic	Placement of processing and memory circuits in peripheral devices of a system as opposed to concentrating all processing and memory circuits in a single, centralized piece of equipment.
Document Assembly	A word processing feature that allows the integration of portions of two or more documents into a single document.
Downtime	The period of time during which personnel or equipment is nonfunctional or inoperative.
Dual-Density Disk	A magnetic storage disk that has twice the storage capacity of a standard disk of the same physical size.
Dvorak Keyboard	A typewriter keyboard designed to take advantage of manual reach and dexterity by placing the most frequently used keys within easy reach of the fingers, thus improving typing speed and accuracy.
EAPROM	Electrically Alterable, Programable Read-Only Memory; a programable read-only memory (see ROM) that can be modified with different instructions or data.

Table 1-1 (continued)

Term	Definition
Field	A defined group or block of data.
Firmware	Electronic devices, such as ROMs, that contain computer program instructions or data.
Floppy Disk (or Flexible Disk)	A thin, flexible magnetic diskette commonly used as a storage medium.
Folio	A page number.
Font	A mechanical or film-strip device used to create printed characters.
Footer	Information located at the bottom of a page, usually used for identification.
Foreground	A word processing function that is apparent to and interacts with the operator.
Front End	A terminal or input device used to create or load data or instructions to a data processing or word processing system.
Front Matter	The information at the front of a document, such as a book or report, including copyright notice, table of contents, list of illustrations, and other similar material.
Full Page	A screenload equivalent to an 8½-by-11-inch text page.
Global Editing Function	An automatic word processing function that interacts with an entire document (data file).
Half Word	Half of a computer word. In a sixteen-bit data word computer, eight bits make up a half word.
Hard Disk	A large, rigid magnetic storage disk.
Hardware	The physical components that comprise electrical and electronic equipment, or the equipment itself.
Hard-Wired	Connected by means of electrical wires or cables.
Header	Information located at the top of a page, usually used for identification or classification of a document.
Human Factors	Parameters used when designing equipment to ensure compatibility with human interaction from both physical and psychological points of view.
Index (plural, indices)	A specific, measurable business indicator used in business modeling.

Table 1-1 (continued)

Term	Definition
Intelligent Copier	A reproduction device capable of receiving digital information (a series of bits) and converting the information into printed copy.
Justification (or Justified Copy)	Alignment of the right-hand margin of text.
Key Bars	Typewriter levers, each having an upper- and lowercase keyboard character, that are mechanically linked to a typewriter key. Key bars strike the paper when a corresponding key is pressed.
Keystroke	The operation of a single key on a typewriter or word processing system keyboard.
Language	A computer instruction language such as ALGOL, BASIC, COBOL, FORTRAN, PASCAL, Assembler, etc.
Leading	Space, measured in units called points, between lines of text. Derived from hot-lead typesetting terminology.
Learning Curve	The graphic plot of individual productivity, which generally shows the benefits of experience. Unit output per unit labor, material, and overhead increases with each successive unit produced. Often called the "experience curve."
Learning Time	The time required for an operator to perform at a fully qualified performance rate. Can be plotted on a learning curve.
Letter-Quality Printer	A printer that produces typewriter-quality print.
Line Illustration	An illustration made from drawn lines, frequently called a line drawing.
Logic	A term used in digital electronics; the basis for computer design.
Look-Up or Substitution Table	A keyboard layout chart used as a guide by a word processing operator to permit the use of standard character keys as special character keys (math, Greek, etc.).
Make-Ready	A term used to describe the preparation process.
Make-Up	The process of preparing a final page for reproduction. Often includes paste-up of text, artwork, page headers

Table 1-1 (continued)

Term	Definition
	and footers, and page numbers. Also called paste-up or page composition.
Mainframe	A term used for a large digital computer system.
Manuscript	The original document prepared by an author.
Mask	A screen-displayed form containing one or more blank areas (or fields) for the operator to fill with appropriate information. In the case of a form letter, the fields can contain name, address, salutation, etc.
Mathpak	A software package that enables a word processing system to perform mathematical computations.
Media-Resident Software	Program instructions and data that reside on changeable media (punched cards, magnetic tape, magnetic disks, etc.)
Medium (plural, Media)	Any material used to store information, including magnetic film, tape, cards, disks, and perforated paper tape and cards.
Memory	A portion of a digital computer used for temporary storage of data.
Menu	A system-generated list of instructions used to guide an operator through the performance of a system function.
Merge	A word processing function that allows mingling of text from two different prefiled locations.
Micrographics	The use of photographic or computer systems to reduce the physical size of documents for convenient storage and retrieval.
Microprocessor	A miniature electronic device containing thousands of active electronic elements on a single chip of silicon, connected to form and function as a digital computer.
Mnemonic	A character or series of characters used to form an instruction for a data processing or word processing system.
Modem	A device used to convert digital data signals to audio signals, or vice versa, and couple those signals between a data processing or word processing system and a telephone system.

Table 1-1 (continued)

Term	Definition
Multifunction System	A word processing system that can perform a variety of tasks, typically including communications and mathematical routines.
Multiple Work Station WP System	A word processing system having two or more operator input terminals.
Nonrecurring Cost	A one-time cost, often incurred at setup or make-ready, that is normally amortized over the life of a process or included as a business overhead expense.
Occupancy	A cost associated with occupying space. Usually includes space, utility, and housekeeping charges.
OCR	Optical Character Reader; a device which scans printed text characters and translates the scanned text into digital intelligence compatible with digital computer devices.
Office of Tomorrow	A term used for a futuristic electronic office where word processing and data processing technologies are combined to improve productivity.
Office System	Any system used in an office environment to perform office functions. Often used to describe an integrated multifunction system.
Off-Line	A function performed on a device not directly connected to a data processing or word processing system.
On-Line	A function performed on a device connected directly to a data processing or word processing system.
Operator	The person responsible for hands-on use of word processing equipment.
Page Composition	*See* Make-Up.
Pagination	A word processing system function used to create and sometimes to number pages within a document.
Paste-Up	*See* Make-Up.
Payback	The financial return on a business investment.
Payback Analysis	A comparison of system savings to system costs. Often compares labor, material, overhead, and productivity variances before and after system acquisition.

Table 1-1 (continued)

Term	Definition
Photocomposition	Typesetting by means of a system that uses photosensitive paper.
Pica	A unit of measure used in typesetting. There are approximately six picas to one inch. Each pica is made up of twelve units of measure called points.
Pitch	A term used in the measurement of standard monospace typewriter characters per inch. For example, "ten pitch" means ten characters per inch on a line of text.
Playout	The process of printing or typing text using a word processor.
Point	A unit of measure used in typesetting. There are approximately seventy-two points per inch or twelve points per pica.
Port	An input, output, or combination input-output connector on a data processing or word processing system.
Printer	An output device used on data processing and word processing systems that provides printed copy on paper.
Print Wheel	A changeable print element used on letter-quality and daisy printers.
Program	A software term used to describe a set of computer instructions.
PROM	Programable Read-Only Memory; a read-only memory (see ROM) that can be programed at the factory with a fixed set of instructions or data.
Prompt	A system message used to assist an operator in performing a system function, to communicate system status, or to inform the operator of an illegal keyboard entry.
Proportional Spacing	A system used in typesetting that allocates units of horizontal measure to characters in proportion to their width.
Protocol	A data transmission signaling code prescribing strict adherence. Examples of protocols include 2270, 2741, 2780, and 3780.

Table 1-1 (continued)

Term	Definition
Queue	*See* Cue.
QWERTY Keyboard	The standard typewriter keyboard configuration in which the top row of letters from the left to right begins Q-W-E-R-T-Y.
Ragged Right	An uneven (unjustified) right-hand margin.
RAM	Random Access Memory; a high-speed semiconductor memory commonly used in data processing and word processing systems.
Read	The retrieval of data from storage media to memory for display, communications, printing, or processing in a data processing or word processing system.
Recurring Cost	A cost (usually including labor, material, and overhead) that is incurred each time a unit is produced or a job or process is performed.
ROM	Read-Only Memory; an unalterable electronic storage device containing computer program instructions or data.
RS-232C	A standard interconnect system with fixed physical and electrical characteristics, used to interface data processing or word processing systems with one another or with other devices in a system.
Screen	A device used to display information on a data processing or word processing system.
Screenload	The maximum amount of text characters which can appear at one time on a data processing or word processing system display. Calculated by multiplying the number of characters per line by the number of lines displayed at one time.
Seize	To use (or gain access to) a dictation device or channel.
Selectric	The name of a typewriter manufactured by IBM which uses a spherical type font.
Software	The media (paper, magnetic tape, etc.) used to store computer programs (instructions). Sometimes includes descriptive documentation.

Table 1-1 (continued)

Term	Definition
Sort	A data processing and word processing function used to arrange information in alphabetical, numerical, or alphanumerical order.
Stand-Alone System	A work station that is independent or can function by itself.
Stop Code	A word processing system operator instruction imbedded in document text that signals the printer to stop. Usually used in conjunction with a type-font change.
Subscript	A character that falls below the baseline (H_2O).
Substitution Table	*See* Look-Up Table.
Superscript	A character that is elevated above the baseline (C^{12}).
System-Resident Software	Program instructions and data which are an integral part of a data processing or word processing system.
Tank Recorder	A tape recording device that uses a large, continuous magnetic tape loop for audio recording.
Tape Drive	A magnetic tape machine equipped with large reels of magnetic tape, often used with a large digital computer system for information storage and retrieval.
Telecommunications	Digital data transmission over a telephone system.
Terminal	Any input or output device connected to a data processing or word processing system.
Text Editing	The act of creating, manipulating, adding, or deleting text characters on a data processing or word processing system.
Thimble Printer	A letter-quality printer used on word processing systems. The thimble printer uses a type font shaped like a thimble.
Tone Illustration	A photographic illustration.
Transparent	A process or function that is unseen by a data processing or word processing system operator.
Trending	A business forecasting method based on historical performance data.

Table 1-1 (continued)

Term	**Definition**
TTY	An abbreviation for teletypewriter communication.
Typesetter	A machine used to set high-quality type. A photocomposer is a typesetter.
VDU	Video Display Unit; *see* Display.
"What If"	A term used by businessmen when looking at potential alternatives.
Word	A full complement of digital data bits.
Work Station	An input terminal used by a word processing system operator.
Write	To transfer data from memory to storage media in a data processing or word processing system.
Zero-Based Budgeting	A business discipline that discounts past organizational and performance trends and establishes new business projections by challenging each business entity and expenditure.

2

The Human Side of Word Processing

2-1. INTRODUCTION

When looking at word processing systems, it's quite easy to restrict your thinking to the equipment, furniture, and software involved while overlooking the people involved. This is a classic and often costly mistake; it most often occurs where an autocratic style of management exists. But people are really the critical part of the system; they must be thoughtfully considered in order to ensure overall successful system performance. Before getting into a discussion of human relations and ways that the people involved can be included in system selection, we'll take a brief look at supervisory style.

People are a vital system element

2-2. SUPERVISORY STYLE

Many supervisors seem to have a knack for being well liked by their subordinates, getting continued high performance from them, and commanding an impressive level of loyalty. Supervisors in this enviable position often differ drastically from one another. But there is normally a common thread—they all like people, and they consider them in their decision-making process. Even though their styles vary, they tell their people what's needed to get the job done, help them with their problems, and recognize them for their efforts. These people can be fundamentally autocratic, democratic, free-rein, or somewhere in between. The autocratic supervisor makes all the decisions, demands full obedience, and therefore had better be right. The democratic manager discusses and consults, draws ideas from others, and lets his people help set policies. The democratic manager gets participation and generates strong teamwork. Free-rein leadership is the most difficult to use, but can be the most effective when used with skill and judgment. Here the manager depends upon the employee's sense of responsibility and good judgment to get things done. Which is best? At different times and with different people, you'll find a need for all three.

Three styles of supervision

No one has a purely autocratic, democratic, or free-rein style. It is important for every manager to recognize that there are as many supervisory styles as there are personalities. And brilliance has no relationship to success as a supervisor. You'll see some extremely bright people who make poor to mediocre supervisors while others, who perhaps lack brilliance, make outstanding supervisors.

What makes a good supervisor

An unthinking, autocratic type of manager will often select the system that he or she believes is best, thrust it upon the people involved, and expect them to adapt to the new-fangled machinery. Since autocratic managers make all the decisions, they are also responsible for being right. When this is the case, everyone, including the manager, is frustrated. The anxiety experienced by those affected by this kind of action is sometimes overwhelming. Many long-time, loyal employees will begin looking for new jobs. The result is often costly employee turnover.

They'd better be right

To avoid this kind of reaction, a lot of thought should go into the human side of the business. When you're contemplating the installation of a new, automated office system, it's important to reflect upon your supervisory style. It's a time to proceed cautiously, involving your people in the thought process. When the decisions are finally made, your people will feel that they are part of those decisions. Before getting into what it takes to involve those who will be affected by a change in equipment or methods, it might be worthwhile to take a look at the organization and how it can be used to help involve those concerned with change.

Involve your people in the process

2-3. THE ORGANIZATION SYSTEM

The formal and informal organization

Most everyone who has taken management courses has heard of the formal and informal organization that exists within a business. The formal organization is the one that appears on the company's organizational chart. There are clear-cut functions and reporting levels, and everyone understands the pecking order. A typical organizational chart is shown in Figure 2-1, which shows how the hypothetical Subterranean Enterprises, Inc., is structured.

The informal organization is not on a chart, but it certainly exists. It's made up of relationships that evolve over the years. The personalities and strengths and weaknesses of people come into play. It's important to understand the informal organization to get things done. If you're concerned with high quality, there are certain individuals you involve in your project. If it's speed you're looking for, then you'll probably choose someone else. Frequently, you find that getting things done through people is based on the art of knowing the right person as well as your skill in interpersonal relations. People who aren't even listed on an organizational chart may get results for you. They often ignore the formal structure, sidestepping organizational bottlenecks, and get to the heart of things in an instant.

Getting results through the right people

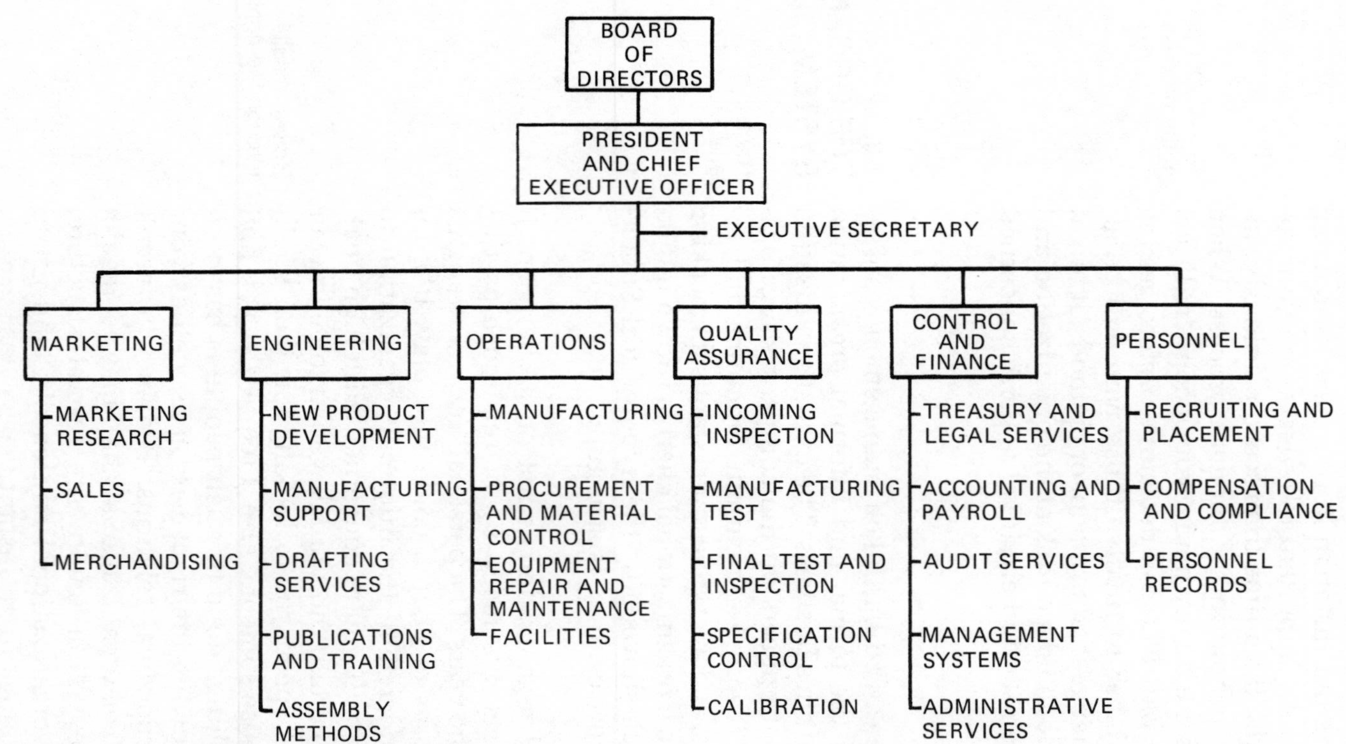

Figure 2-1. Organizational Chart, Subterranean Enterprises, Inc.

For example, if you need a rush copy in the print shop, it may be necessary to avoid the production control clerk, sneak by the print shop supervisor, and go directly to the foreman, Joe, who's a "good old boy." You can engage Joe in a "bull session" about the weekend ball game, buy him a cup of coffee, and say "Oh, by the way, do you think you could get me a few copies of this little job?" Joe slips the work to one of his printers for instant processing. When Joe hands you the finished job, you spend an extra minute talking about the condition of the infield, thank him profusely, and head for the door—mission accomplished.

This kind of activity exists when the formal system doesn't work well. When the informal organization becomes the only one that works, then there are serious problems in the formal one. Often those up the ladder don't understand the processes involved in the job, have no idea of what the inefficiencies are costing the business, don't really want to be bothered with them, and may dodge involvement entirely.

The organization that works

What happens in this kind of organization when new, computer-based technology is mentioned? When "Old Deadwood" is confronted with new technology, including word processing systems, he becomes threatened.

"What's wrong with the way things are?" he may say. "Everything's under control, isn't it? Why should we go through all the trouble of having to learn something new that probably won't work anyway?"

Sidestepping change is natural

If Old Deadwood can sidestep change, he will. This lets him continue to do exactly what he does best—nothing. Figure 2-2 could be the informal organization, which is how things really happen at Subterranean Enterprises.

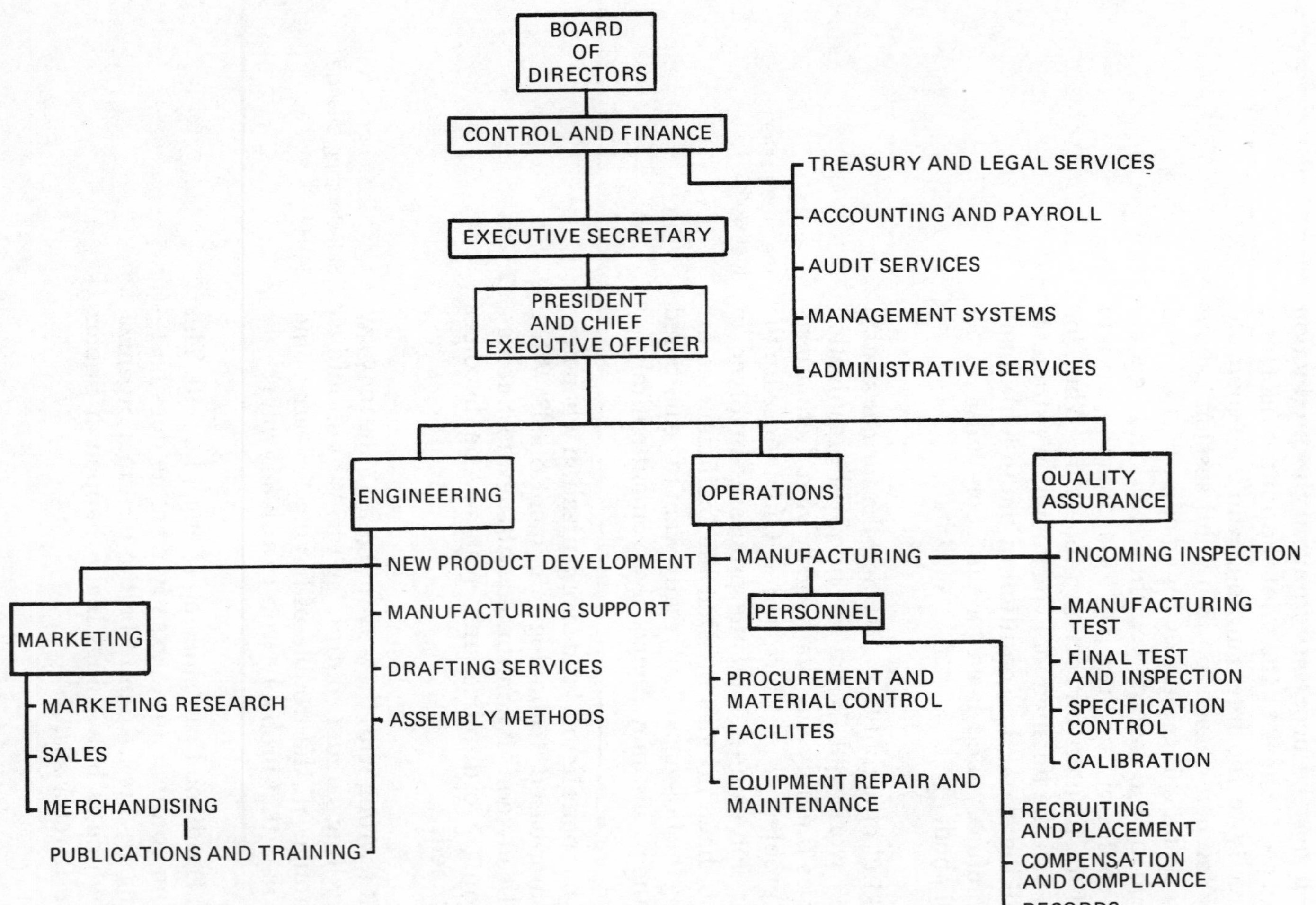

Figure 2-2. Informal Organization, Subterranean Enterprises, Inc.

2-4. RESTRUCTURING FOR EFFICIENCY: BENEFITS AND PITFALLS

Restructuring a trauma

Restructuring is often a trauma for everyone involved. But trauma can be minimized if the right approach is taken. This section discusses the natural resistance to change and then looks at two approaches to change. The first is the wrong way to bring about change; this is the way that we often see it happen. The second is the ideal; it rarely happens this way.

2-5. The Natural Resistance to Change

Fear of the unknown

When something new comes along, people are frequently suspicious. There is a tendency to want to cling to the familiar, more comfortable way of doing things. New methods are viewed with suspicion. There is a fear of the unknown, a fear of failure, and sometimes a reluctance to put forth the extra effort required to learn new skills. Managers often suspect that their people are stubborn and lazy when they seem unwilling to learn new methods. But what may appear to be stubbornness is quite often deep-rooted anxiety. People may perceive new ways as the threat of personal obsolescence: they are being put to a test. If they have difficulty learning to work with a new type of equipment or system, they may not survive their jobs. If the job is changed as the result of an organization change, they may find themselves in a hostile environment. The preponderance of negative implications associated with change normally outweighs the positive ones.

Negatives outweigh the positives

It is imperative for a manager to "sell" change to his people. When the "tell" approach is used, everyone seems to find a thousand reasons why things won't work and not one reason why it will. When the "sell" approach is used, all the good reasons must be brought to the forefront in the beginning. Some typical positive benefits include

1. Fun in learning new things
2. Easier and more productive jobs
3. Opportunity for special training
4. Increased responsibility and corresponding job growth
5. Interesting and more interesting jobs
6. Opportunities for personal advancement
7. Better company performance through increased productivity
8. Improved job security.

Positive benefits

All of these and more can be used as positive motivators for the people involved. Of course there's a lot more to merchandising change than discussing benefits. The changes must make sense. They must yield the intended result. They must be researched thoroughly, and all the right questions must be asked. Last, but of prime importance, they must involve the people affected by the change. To illustrate our discussion, let's take a look at a few cases of how change might be instituted.

2-6. The Way It Shouldn't Happen. The president of Subterranean Enterprises decides that the only way they are going to increase their profitability and improve customer service is through automation. The cost of labor is rising rapidly. The manufacturing operations are benefiting dramatically from new, high-volume equipment and processes. Now it's time to look at administrative areas. Fully sixty percent of the company's manpower is in the office. This includes marketing, planning, finance, procurement, engineering, documentation, personnel, and public relations. The manager of administrative services is called in.

The mood is right to automate

"The opportunity for increased productivity and greater company profits is in your hands. Go look at the manufacturing operations. They've been automating for years. Now it's your turn. I'm behind you a hundred percent. I want increased productivity, and I want it as soon as possible. The only way we're going to survive in this 'dog-eat-dog' business is through greater productivity in every area. The leverage in administrative and staff functions can be tremendous."

It's your turn

The administrative services manager never dreamed he would find the funding, let alone the personal backing of the president, to install new office systems. He knows exactly what the president is talking about. He's been reading all about modern office products and centralized word processing centers. But they've always been out of reach. Support functions have always been last when the money was being passed out. A chance at last! He's prepared to give it a whirl. New equipment is needed. To complement centralization and the new equipment, the reporting structure must be modified, and the office space must be rearranged.

A chance at last

The manager telephones some word processing and dictation equipment vendors, looks at the equipment with less than full understanding, looks at the price tags with apprehension, and picks one based on price and reputation of the vendor. These guys have been around for a while and should be as good as anybody.

Shopping for a system

Now that the equipment has been selected, the next step is to figure out where to put it and who should get to use it. The manager goes over the new layout with the facilities department.

Deciding where to place the system

"We're going to centralize administrative services. Automatic text processors and new dictation equipment will be installed. We're reducing the number of secretaries; they'll be relocated to the new word processing center. Centralization is the key to greater productivity."

Centralization must be the key

Put the junior people in word processing

Now that the furniture and floor space is planned, changes in personnel assignments are analyzed. The senior secretaries will continue to support upper level management personnel. The newer ones will be reassigned to the central operation.

A stroke of genius

The manager who decides on the new structure and understands the rationale for change is often quite glib. It should be obvious to everyone through a casual examination of the two-paragraph memo describing the change. After all, the new equipment, new layout, and reporting structure constitute a stroke of genius.

Reviewing the plan

The administrative services manager makes an appointment to go over the master plan with the president. He nervously races through the volumes of material, showing equipment brochures, office layouts, reassignments, and anticipated improvements as the president looks on in a daze.

"You've done a lot of work. It looks like a good plan. Let's call my people together and explain it to them."

He seems to know exactly what he's doing

The meeting is called. The administrative services manager goes through the material once more. It's a little smoother this time; he seems to know exactly what he's talking about, and the use of a lot of technical terms is impressive. The assembled managers are uncomfortable, but they really aren't sure why. The president seems to understand everything that the administrative services manager is saying. They're certainly not going to embarrass themselves by asking what could be a stupid question.

They reluctantly agree

The part about taking away secretaries from some of their people could be a problem. They anticipate some trouble here, but a little sacrifice in hard times comes with the territory. The managers reluctantly agree to the plan. The administrative services manager sighs in relief. He's won.

As soon as the memo is circulated, the murmur of disgruntled voices can be heard along the corridors. The murmur builds to a crescendo of despair. There are loud arguments, gnashing teeth, tears, resignations. The administrative services manager sees people shaking their heads in disbelief whenever he looks up from his desk.

The result: disaster

Where did he go wrong? Let's look at another approach to restructuring the office.

2-7. The Way It Should Happen. The president of Subterranean Enterprises decides that the only way they are going to increase their profitability and improve customer service is through automation. The cost of labor is rising rapidly. The manufacturing operations are benefiting dramatically from new, high-volume equipment and processes. Now it's time to look at administrative areas. Fully sixty percent of the company's manpower is in the office. This includes marketing, planning, finance, procurement, engineering, documentation, personnel, and public relations. The manager of administrative services is called in.

The mood is right to automate

"The opportunity for increased productivity and greater company profits is in your hands. Go look at the manufacturing operations. They've been automating for years. Now it's your turn. I'm behind you a hundred percent. I want increased productivity, and I want it as soon as possible. The only way we're going to survive in this 'dog-eat-dog' business is through greater productivity in every area. The leverage in administrative and staff functions can be tremendous."

It's your turn

The administrative services manager never dreamed he would find the funding, let alone the personal backing of the president, to install new office systems. He knows exactly what the president is talking about. He's been reading all about modern office

A chance at last

products and centralized word processing centers. But they've always been out of reach. Support functions have always been last when the money was being passed out. A chance at last!

Enlisting help

Although the administrative services manager has some ideas, he decides to do some strategy work. He realizes that those affected by changes in equipment and organization should be involved from the very beginning. The payoff will be commitment to change. When they participate in the decision-making process, they become much more dedicated to making the changes work.

The plan

The administrative services manager outlines his plan.

1. Call a meeting of the people involved.
2. Discuss productivity as related to the success of the business and their personal success in a company that could survive in a competitive environment.
3. Announce the opportunity to streamline their operations through the installation of new tools.
4. Form teams of employees to look at specific areas for improvement. Each must be given clear objectives:
   a. Review processes and equipment currently being used and identify possible improvements through eliminating wasted steps, combining similar activities, avoiding unnecessary delays, and reducing material usage.
   b. Investigate modern equipment and methods available for use in upgrading existing functions, including costs and peculiar installation considerations.
   c. Review the administrative support organization's functional responsibilities in the search for cost-effective improvements.

5. Upon approval of the recommendations, form a scheduling committee made up of members from each team to schedule the changes.

The administrative services manager makes an appointment with the president and explains his strategy. The first phase is communicating the problems to the people involved. The next phase is getting the people involved in the planning and research. Phase three is selection and implementation, which continues to include heavy participation of the people affected. Sure, it would be easier to do the planning and research without enlisting the people concerned, but the implementation could be a major failure if they are simply "bulldozed" into change.

Reviewing the plan

The president agrees. "You've got your work cut out for you, but I like your plan. I like your getting the people involved early. It should help the whole thing work much better. I'll call a staff meeting, and we'll tell everyone what we're about to do."

The staff meeting is a success. A few managers are not confident that their people will be much help, but since the president is for it, they'll back it all the way.

A few days later the administrative services manager calls a meeting of the people involved. In the meeting the administrative services manager spends a significant amount of time explaining the tough business environment. The discussion includes information about competitors' market share, pricing, how profit is made, the percentage of profit absorbed by payroll, and how cost reduction relates to job security and company growth.

Tying cost reduction to employee security

The portion on modern equipment is extremely positive; new equipment and processes mean an opportunity for all employees to enlarge their skills. It will be an excellent experience as well as fun learning

The equipment described positively

how to use modern, new equipment. In addition, everyone's job will be made easier.

The administrative services manager explains the purpose of the teams. As the teams are formed, the participants are enthusiastic. Membership includes people from different areas who have never worked together. Each team has a leader responsible for calling meetings and keeping a record of team activity.

Forming teams

Once the teams are formed, their activity is monitored and encouraged by the administrative services manager. Supervisors are also involved in supporting the team activity, providing the necessary resources, and encouraging progress according to a predetermined schedule.

Supervisory encouragement

Upon completion of the team projects, the team leaders present their findings in a special meeting. The administrative services manager commends each for its contribution. He explains that each team will stay intact during the entire installation and start-up phase.

The "no-surprise," participative team activity not only helps sell change, it guarantees early success. The people involved are part of the decision and therefore motivated to promote successful implementation.

The people participate

2-8. Some Concluding Comments

The two cases described above are at opposite ends of a spectrum covering what can happen when searching for a way to improve productivity in the office. In both cases, the administrative services manager had good intentions. However, in the first case he coupled limited analysis, minimum systems knowledge, and poor planning with disregard for the people involved. The result was organizational

Good intentions alone don't guarantee success

breakdown. In the second case, the manager recognized his personal limitations and showed concern for the people affected. The time spent in strategic planning, selling the benefits, and involving the people in system analysis work led to a successful installation.

People make it work

Recognizing the need for improved performance, establishing a good set of objectives, developing well-thought-out strategies, and involving the people at all stages are the key ingredients to successful system selection, organization, and implementation. Great attention to detail is necessary for a system to work well, because the system is really a great number of bits and pieces that must all be combined into a well-coordinated, synchronized universe. And at the very heart of the system are people. It is entirely within their power to make the system work or fail.

2-9. SELECTING AND KEEPING WORD PROCESSING OPERATORS

Good people of all kinds are hard to find today. When you do find them, they're often hard to keep. Today's work force is transient, and perhaps word processing system operators are among the most transient. Competition for good WP operators is fierce for several reasons. These include

Competition for good WP operators

1. A large, growing job market
2. Increasing WP operator wage scales
3. Natural attrition (personal reasons, illness, etc.).

How do you find and hold good WP operators? Let's look at where WP operators come from and some of the reasons people change jobs or leave the work force. This information may help you find the right places to look for WP operators as well as help to develop a checklist of what questions to ask during initial employment interviews. You may also want to review your compensation policies if you suspect they are not competitive.

2-10. Selecting Word Processing Operators

The WP industry is growing by leaps and bounds. There are around one hundred WP system manufacturers in the U.S. plus numerous peripheral equipment and supply companies. Tens of thousands of new WP terminals are being installed annually. Each terminal represents a workstation for a WP operator. The demand exceeds the supply. This is the environment you're in when faced with the prospect of finding a WP operator. It's a seller's market.

Demand exceeds supply

Selecting WP operators is really an oversimplification—it connotes identifying the best operator from a large list of candidates. The fact of the matter is that you have to find the operator first. If you find two, then you can begin the selection process. In looking for operators, there are three important sources. These are

Find them one at a time

1. New graduates from schools and colleges
2. WP operators currently in the work force
3. Secretarial and clerical personnel in the work force.

2-11. New Graduates. This source is the smallest. Only a trickle of WP operators are graduating from community schools and colleges, making but a drop in the supply bucket. In addition to being small in number, they often have no work experience and find it difficult to adjust to a new, no-nonsense work environment. Those who are directly out of school often have little more than some fundamental keyboard training. Understanding what's required in a particular, "real world" business environment is rare for at least two reasons. First, each business is different. The finance sector will have demands different from those of a legal organization. A first-in, first-out word processing center will have a completely different

Are they really ready?

approach to word processing than a process-oriented publications production shop. Second, many poorly funded, ill-equipped labs and out-of-touch curriculums do not provide WP operators with exposure to up-to-date equipment or instill the proper expectations for a career in word processing. Those who are surprised by their new WP environment are often disillusioned and quickly become turnover statistics.

Others who may qualify for consideration are graduates of business schools or holders of associate degrees in secretarial science. Many of these people have not considered a career in word processing and are sometimes surprised to find an opportunity in the field. Recent graduates will most often be young, unsettled, undergoing a change in personal life style, and uncertain about their career. When they are in this phase of their life, you shouldn't count on keeping them more than a year or two. Of course, there are always happy exceptions. But experience shows that marriage, a husband's job move, starting a family, and other influences typical among young people make early turnover a high probability.

Turnover
a high probability

2-12. Operators Currently in the Work Force. WP operators currently in the work force usually come from some other company; they may also, however, be people returning to the work force after relocation or raising a family. Whatever the circumstances, these will normally be the most experienced operators. They'll run down the learning curve (attain productivity expectations) the fastest. An important question to ask people in this category is why they left their last job. If they spend excessive time in bitter criticism of their former employer, watch out! They could be trouble. If they are complimentary about their last job, they probably had a good relationship with their supervisor and coworkers and will blend well with your people and job environment.

Listen to what they say

2-13. Upgrading Secretarial and Clerical Personnel. Secretarial and clerical personnel currently in the work force make up a large, often excellent supply of WP operators. When at your wits' end to find someone to operate your equipment, you may be pleasantly surprised to find that a sharp secretary or clerk with good keyboard skills can fit right into a WP slot with a little encouragement and training. I've seen people in this category turn into top WP operators within a year. The importance of intelligence and keyboard skills cannot be overemphasized. Bright people are quicker to understand word processing system concepts. They tend to maximize system features and devise new, simpler methods for doing things. People with good keyboard skills usually like to type. This is essential in word processing. A good keyboard person can make a WP system "sing." I've seen some who can run two magnetic card-based machines simultaneously over an entire eight-hour shift and enjoy it.

Intelligence and keyboard skills needed

2-14. Keeping Word Processing Operators

WP operators are usually sharp people. They have contact with vendor representatives, join word processing associations, chat with fellow WP operators at training classes and seminars, and monitor vendor sales and support representatives in order to "keep their ear to the ground" for better job opportunities. This is particularly true of WP operators who have been converted from secretarial or clerical positions and trained on the job. When they become fully qualified, watch out! They become quite aware of what their new-found skills are worth.

They know what they're worth

2-15. Pay Them What They're Worth. The tendency of most managers is to move newly trained or converted WP operators along slowly. For example, it may take several years for a convertee to reach the going salary rate. If they are being held back, they may become quite aggressive in searching for a new, better-paying job opportunity. The advice here is to pay them what they're worth.

Dragging your feet will likely end in the loss of a good worker. Although they may have only a few months' or a year's experience in word processing, they will be familiar with company operations. This knowledge coupled with their new skill is usually valuable to you. Don't sell them short; if you do, you'll be the one to pay by starting from scratch with a new trainee.

Don't sell them short

2-16. Stay on Top of the Market Rate. There are a number of advantages to staying abreast of going salary rates in your business. These include

1. Knowing what the competition is paying for similar labor functions
2. Holding on to your people through reasonable compensation
3. Demonstrating to your employees that you maintain competitive rates.

There's no substitute for wage surveys. In large companies with sizable staffs, your compensation manager should be able to obtain wage analysis information in the local labor market. Information is usually obtained through agreements with similar businesses in the area. It is organized by generic job classification, including levels of proficiency. To make the most of these surveys, it's important to have good job descriptions in order to obtain "apples-to-apples" comparisons.

Wage surveys a must

Another source of wage survey information is nationwide wage surveys that are published in a number of national magazines. This kind of information is sometimes of little value in areas where the economy is at either end of the national average. An hourly job in Melbourne, Florida or Austin, Texas will demand less compensation than a similar one in San Francisco or Boston. Therefore, local survey information is critical for both employer and employee. If you are in a unique economy and your company is not engaged in a wage survey group, it will likely be helpful to monitor your personnel applications for wages paid at previous jobs. You can also include a discussion about wages in employee exit interviews. If they are leaving for an increase in pay, they will often be eager to tell you about a good raise, if for no other reason than to rub your nose in it.

Local information key

If your people recognize your interest in providing competitive compensation, they will usually consider you to be a fair employer. It's valuable to let them know that you are keeping track of going rates in the market. Not only does this give them a sense of security about their pay, it may also alleviate their curiosity to seek out wage information on their own. Not that this is bad, but there's always the chance that they'll obtain bad information or even find a new job in the process. Even when jobs are not available at what they believe to be the going rate, they can become dissatisfied with their present job, believing you're taking advantage of them.

Show your interest

2-17. Other Compensation. When thinking about compensation on the job, we must also include benefits. This includes such things as

Benefits

- Vacation
- Holidays
- Sick leave
- Paid personal time off
- Insurance
- Pension
- Profit sharing

- Working hours
- Facility quality
- Educational assistance and training
- Recreation programs.

Most of these benefits are determined by what a company can afford to provide in its business environment. Of course, some are more expensive than others. Let's look briefly at a few of the items that can be controlled through thoughtful management.

Regular hours of work

Hours of work should be kept to a regular, no-surprise level. When overtime is required, it should be communicated as far in advance as possible. Regularly springing overtime on people who often have other plans for the end of their shift can become an intolerable condition. If overtime is a rule instead of an exception, your staff is too small. You should either add permanent people or use a temporary agency to get you over the hump.

Keep the area clean

The quality of your facility is important. People have to spend a minimum of eight hours each day in their work area. It should be clean, well lighted, and temperature-controlled; where impact printers are used, acoustic covers, noise reduction panels, carpeting and perhaps drapes can be installed to keep the sound below an annoying level. Cleanliness is one of the most visible barometers of mangement. A manager who lets his area become dirty shows a lack of concern for the people who have to work there. Dirty areas are both unproductive and unsafe. Work is buried, tools are misplaced, and clutter often turns into tripping and fire hazards. Clean areas, on the other hand, are normally organized to do the job. Everything has a place and is easily found. Work in progress is organized by category or neatly staged for the next operation. The people in a clean work area will be more efficient, more productive, and certainly more content with working conditions.

One final comment about quality of supervision is probably appropriate. The supervisor of an operation is the single most vital element to its continued success. It is imperative to have qualified supervisors who get along with and command the respect of the work force. Regardless of how good a company might be in terms of pay, benefits, and facility quality, the people will be unhappy if the supervision is poor. Your supervisors should be individuals who are, first, interested in people, and, second, trained in supervisory fundamentals. There are a number of good supervisory training courses available. You owe it to both yourself and your people to ensure that all supervisors are well trained. The productivity of your people and the success of your business are at stake. Not only does training help prepare people to handle day-to-day problems, it also helps them to recognize that supervision is an important professional discipline that must be developed through education, experience, and hard work.

Supervisor training is important

3

Word Processing Systems: Yesterday, Today, and Tomorrow

3-1. INTRODUCTION

Before getting into a review of where word processing systems came from, where they are today, and where they are going, it may be well to define the term "word processing system" in the context of this book. We'll use "word processing" to refer to any machine or group of machines used to store, manipulate, and give out information. The information is in a form that is easily interpreted by the user, that is, in commonly understood words. In a broad sense, this definition can apply to systems that process words in either written or spoken form. By this definition, then, a typewriter or a tape recorder both qualify as word processing systems.

Word processing defined

This chapter provides only a brief overview of the evolution and direction of word processing systems. To spend a great deal of time on historical trivia and speculation is not productive, particularly for a busy business manager whose primary interest is the bottom line.

3-2. TYPING SYSTEMS

The typing system uses a keyboard that is either mechanically or electrically linked to an output or storage device. For example, the original mechanical typewriter used a mechanical linkage system that connected the character keys on the keyboard to type bars. When a key was pressed down by the operator, a corresponding type bar forced grease-impregnated ribbon against paper, transferring the character image from the key bar. In a modern electronic word processing system, the character keys are most often electrically coupled to storage media or electronic memory. When a key is pressed by the operator, a corresponding electrical signal is generated, causing a data code representing the character key pressed to be stored on a magnetic medium, such as a magnetic tape or disk, in an electronic memory circuit, on the screen of a video display tube, or in some cases, a combination of these.

Keyboards a common element

3-3. Manual Typewriters

The original manual typing machines were primitive in design, had a relatively slow response time, and were operated primarily by men because it took a good deal of physical force to press the character keys down. After the key was released, gravity was responsible for letting the key fall away from the paper. This was so slow that a great deal of research went into the design of the keyboard to ensure that it was time-consuming to use. The development of an efficient keyboard on which the most frequently used characters were located together beneath the fingers with the most dexterity proved to be problematic: an efficient design increased the potential for key jams and made typing awkward. Hence the QWERTY keyboard, as we know it today, was developed to slow typing-machine operators down. The characters Q-W-E-R-T-Y are the first six characters on the top alphabetical row of the keyboard and are commonly used to refer to the standard typewriter keyboard.

Primitive design

Efficient design a problem

Several new, more efficient keyboards have been designed over the years, particularly since typewriters have increased reaction times dramatically. Many are completely electronic, and their response times are literally millionths of a second. The designs include both rearrangement of the keys for more efficient access and contouring the keyboard to conform more closely to the shape of the hand.

Better keyboard design improves speed

The Dvorak keyboard is perhaps the most widely accepted new keyboard design. It has been around for a number of years and has proven to be much more efficient than the QWERTY design. However, since almost all typists are taught QWERTY, Dvorak has not made substantial gains. A number of keyboard manufacturers offer Dvorak as an option, but few are sold. Many proponents of the Dvorak system state that operators can become proficient on the Dvorak system in a few short weeks. Their speeds can double that of the QWERTY keyboard speed, and they can easily transfer back and forth between QWERTY and Dvorak keyboards without difficulty. In other words, they don't lose their QWERTY skills when they master the Dvorak system.

The Dvorak keyboard

3-4. Electric Typewriters

Electric typewriters made substantial improvements in machine response time, permitting increased typing speed. The first electric typewriters used mechanical linkages and key bars. There are still some typebar electric typewriters manufactured today: IBM's Executive line uses typebars. One of the earliest nontypebar typewriters was the IBM Selectric. Extremely popular today, this machine uses a spherical type font, which looks like a ball. Type characters are located in horizontal and vertical rows around the type font, which shifts so as to correspond to the pressed key before it strikes the ribbon. Whereas typebar units employ a moving carriage so that the platen and paper pass from left to right beneath the

Improved response time increases output

typebar impact position, Selectric typewriters use a carrier. The carrier moves the type font and ribbon from left to right. The fixed platen rolls to advance the paper.

The early manual and electric typewriters only enabled operators to transfer type onto paper. Corrections, or "text editing," was done either by retyping an entire page of text or by using erasers, correction fluid, or the "cut and paste" method. The advent of electronic typing systems made text editing much easier.

3-5. Electronic Typing Systems

In this section we'll look briefly at the evolution of electronic typing systems, their storage media, and the concept of "memory."

3-6. Magnetic Media Systems. Some of the earliest so-called electronic typing systems were commercially available in the mid-1960s. These systems used magnetic tape as a storage medium, where typed information was coded on magnetic tape. This method was similar to recording information on a tape recorder.

Storing words on tape

The earliest systems allowed the operator to strike over errors simply by entering a new code over the existing one. Dual-tape units allowed operators to transfer information from one tape to another and to insert typed corrections where desired. For example, if a document consisted of three paragraphs, and the middle paragraph required substantial changes, the operator could transfer the first paragraph to a new tape, manually type the paragraph to be corrected, "skipping" the original second paragraph, and finally transfer the last paragraph to the new tape intact. Once the tape was ready, the machines could play out typewritten material at over 150 words per minute. Following the tape units were magnetic card

Playout exceeds 150 wpm

systems, which use magnetic cards instead of tape as a storage medium.

The card systems work much like the tape systems as far as strikeovers, information transfer, multiple playout, and machine speed are concerned. Both systems are extremely productive in applications such as form letters and legal letters, where the same text is used many times. Many of these systems are in use today.

Other magnetic media are also in use today, including a variety of magnetic disks. Some of these, called *minidisks,* are no more than five inches in diameter. One popular type, called *floppy disks* or *flexible disks,* is eight inches in diameter and is used extensively by many word processing system and computer system manufacturers. There are also large, hard disks capable of storing millions of bits of information that are used in word processing systems for text storage. In addition to magnetic disks, magnetic tape and tape cassettes are in use. Information access time for tape is longer than for disks; therefore, tape-based systems are normally slower than disk-based systems, making tape less popular from an operational point of view. However, cassettes are normally inexpensive and easily attainable. The economics of a cassette system are often attractive to small businesses and individuals with small budgets.

3-7. Electronic Memory Systems. Electronic memory typewriters became available in the early 1970s. These systems are capable of storing keystrokes in a "volatile" memory. The term *volatile* means that the memory must have power applied to retain information. If power is interrupted or turned off, the memory is erased. The memory acts like a storage medium where text corrections or document format adjustments can be made. Response time is instantaneous. The disadvantage to a limited, volatile mem-

Storing keystrokes in memory

ory system is that once documents are created and stored in the memory, corrections must be made and the document played out before a new document can be created. The electronic memory typewriter works well in some applications where the document cycle time is rapid from start to finish. Where there are a number of documents that must be processed in parallel, the electronic memory system can become quite awkward.

3-8. DISPLAY-BASED WORD PROCESSING SYSTEMS

Display-based word processing systems began to catch on in the mid-1970s. These systems added a display screen, or cathode ray tube, to word processing. Before the display-based systems, text could only be examined in hard copy form (printed on paper). With the advent of the new system, the word processing operator could view text on a display screen. The text could be modified by means of text-editing features, such as strikeover, insert, and delete commands, and be made letter-perfect before committing the text to paper. The display-based system made text editing much simpler than previous systems, where changes could only be made after a typed copy was available.

Changes without paper

Before getting into a discussion of different types of display-based systems, you should know that there are a variety of technologies used for displaying characters. The majority of display-based systems use cathode ray tubes. Some use small strip, or "window," displays which allow operators to view from approximately a dozen to sixty characters and spaces. Other types of displays in use include liquid crystal, light-emitting diode, and plasma display technologies. However, cathode ray tube (CRT) technology, which has been used in television for years, is well established and the most successful to date. Regardless of the technology used, the main criteria for selection should be

A variety of display technologies

1. The display should support a full assortment of characters, numbers, and punctuation marks. (Some support special symbols.)
2. The display characters must be easy to read.
3. The display must be comfortable to view so as not to cause operator fatigue.
4. The display should have operator controls for brightness, contrast, etc.
5. The display face should minimize stray light reflection.

Display selection criteria

In addition to different display technologies, there are full-page, partial-page, and even two-page displays. A full-page display is normally equivalent to an 8½-by-11-inch sheet of paper. Partial-page displays can be anywhere from six to eight lines to a half page. Two-page displays contain information equivalent to two full-page screenloads. As a rule, large displays cost more than small ones. For example, a full-page display will cost more than a partial-page display.

Display sizes

The decision as to which configuration is best is up to you. All display configurations, as well as non-display word processing systems, are being used productively. It is for you to analyze whether there is truly a performance advantage from one display size to another in your particular application. An approach to analysis that may be helpful is presented in Chapter 8.

3-9. Stand-Alone Systems

The term *stand-alone system* refers to a work station that is totally independent or can function by itself. A typewriter is a stand-alone system in the simplest sense. It is completely independent. Its operator can function in an isolated area and has complete machine control without reliance on devices located in other areas or controlled by other people. The device is a functioning entity unto itself. There are many kinds of stand-alone word processing systems. These range from typewriters without sophisticated electronic circuits or storage capability—that is, the ability to capture and retain keystrokes for later use—to highly complex systems using computer technology, mass storage devices, display screens, and communications capability. Modern electronic stand-alone systems are normally comprised of an input unit (keyboard and display screen), control and memory electronics, storage device (magnetic card, tape, or disk), and an output device (typewriter or letter-quality printer). Figure 3-1 contains a diagram of a typical stand-alone word processing system. Note the cutaway showing some of the electronic circuit cards often found in a word processing system.

For isolated job functions

3-10. Shared-Logic Systems

Shared-logic word processing systems share central control and memory circuitry. The control circuitry, often termed the *central processing unit,* or CPU, is at the heart of a computer system. Here, control of information being processed by the system is accomplished. The memory circuits temporarily store information to be manipulated. The CPU, responding to operator commands, transfers information in and out of memory to a storage device for later use, an output unit such as a printer, or a communications port for transmission to another system. A simplified diagram of a shared-logic system is shown in Figure 3-2. The central control unit of the system is basically a digital computer. It contains a CPU, memory, an arithmetic logic unit (which performs mathematical routines), and input-output (I/O) circuits.

Sharing central control

The term *logic* comes from the field of digital electronics; logic is the basis for digital computer design.

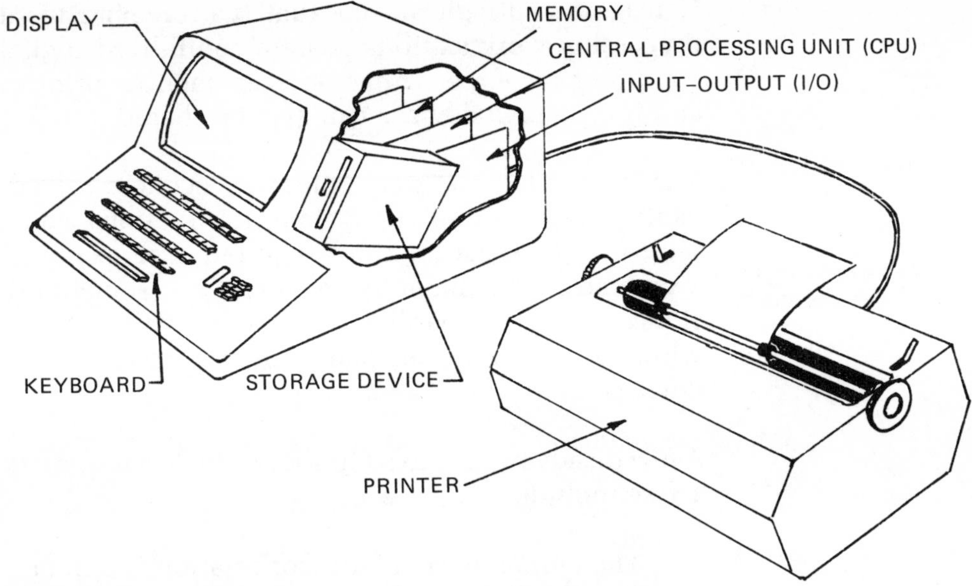

Figure 3-1. A Stand-Alone Word Processing System

Figure 3-2. A Shared-Logic Word Processing System

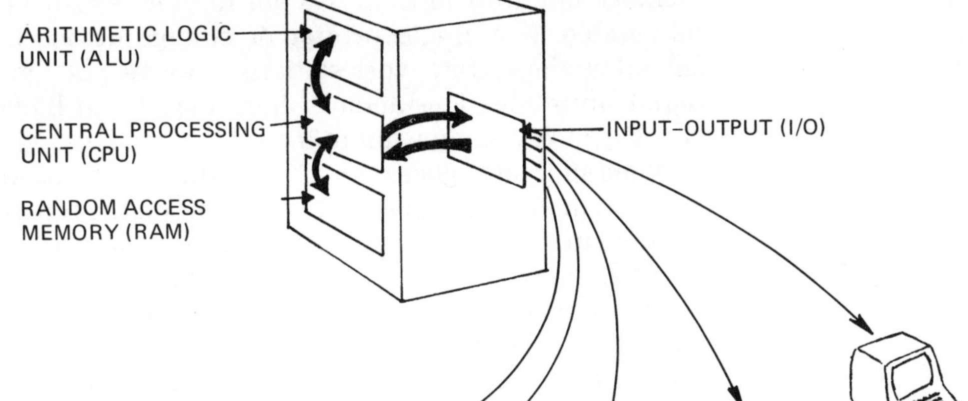

Hence, shared-logic means that two or more word processing work stations share a centralized digital computer resource. Other devices such as printers and text storage devices can also be shared.

Sharing resources reduces costs

The shared-logic system offers an economical advantage over stand-alone systems in situations where multiple work stations are required. For example, a common CPU, memory, printer, and, sometimes, storage device can be shared by several work stations, which are usually keyboard–display screen input devices.

A few disadvantages

A few disadvantages exist in shared-logic equipment. These include

1. The vulnerability of all work stations upon failure of a single system component
2. Response-time degradation as more work-stations are installed on the system.

"Back-up" a good policy

The first disadvantage can be critical in some cases. If the shared-logic system's power supply, CPU, or memory circuitry fail, all system functions will be inoperable. If a single printer or storage device is shared by the system work stations, they may be rendered unusable. The defense here may be to have "back-up." You may want to install two shared-logic systems so if one "goes down," the other can be used to finish those "hot" jobs that can't wait on the repair technician. Another approach is to have a compatible stand-alone machine that uses the same storage media. In some cases this may be the most inexpensive way to provide back-up, depending on your work station requirements. If you're in a large company that has a staff of equipment repair and maintenance technicians, you may want to develop them as a resource in support of your word processing system maintenance needs. Many word processing system companies offer technician training and spare parts. The key is to ensure that they are committed to rapid response to system problems. In any case, you'll have to put a pencil to it to determine the best solution for your particular situation. You'll find some tips in this area in Chapters 8 and 10.

The second disadvantage, response-time degradation, can be aggravating to operators who are used to a system that has been providing them with "instant" response. As work stations are added to a shared-logic system, the system resources (CPU and memory) must work harder to keep up with the demands of the operators. The operators will note that their system becomes increasingly sluggish in response to their keystrokes as more and more work stations are tied in. If they are sharing a single printer, they may begin to find conflict when queueing up documents to be typed. Some shared-logic system manufacturers only offer a maximum of two work stations per CPU, so here your options are limited for you. However, many shared-logic system manufacturers offer four to eight work stations, and some claim even more can be successfully used. Here again, there is a logical way to determine how many terminals are optimal and how many and what type of printers are needed to support the business activity. And above all, don't believe everything your salesperson tells you; check it out for yourself.

Overloading can be a problem

3-11. Distributed-Logic Systems

A simplified diagram of a distributed-logic system is shown in Figure 3-3. The distributed-logic system uses the same basic components as the shared-logic system except that portions of the control and memory circuits are distributed out of a central electronics package to the work stations. This allows many of the simple editing functions to be achieved locally, within the work station itself. By taking total reliance away from a single, centrally located CPU and memory, the distributed-logic system provides improved operator response time (or system speed). There is

Better response time

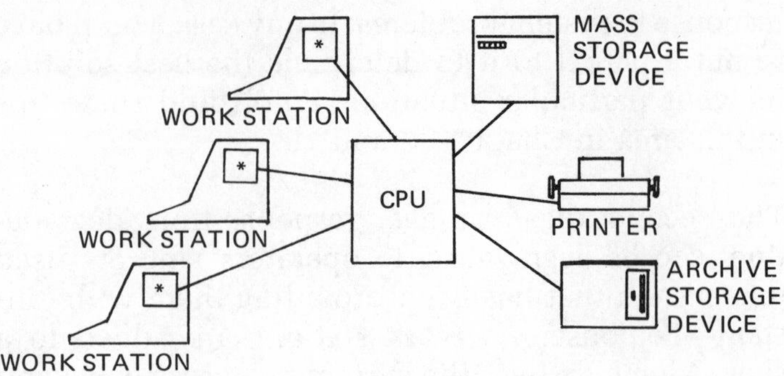

Figure 3-3. A Distributed-Logic Word Processing System

less degradation in response time as additional work stations are added to a distributed-logic system. When deciding how many printers or storage devices to use on a distributed-logic system, the same rationale that applies to a shared-logic system can be used for a distributed-logic system.

3-12. Timeshare and Mainframe Systems

Using existing equipment for word processing

Another approach that has been taken to word processing is the use of the company's existing computer resource, which may be a timeshare service or an owned central computer. Most large computer manufacturers offer word processing or text-editing packages. With the proper terminals and computer software, existing computer resources can be used for text editing. There are a few drawbacks to this approach. These include

Some potential drawbacks

1. Full-time availability for word processing
2. Letter-quality printer output
3. Interface to supporting systems such as typesetters.

The first drawback occurs when priority is given to data processing activity. When this happens, personnel designated for word processing must often wait in line to use the timeshared resource.

The second drawback is encountered when the word processing people are stuck with data processing output devices. Line and matrix printers commonly used for data processing output are of poor quality. This drawback can be overcome when a letter-quality printer is installed for word processing support.

The third drawback is a problem related to the specific system that the company is tied to. Most telecommunications packages used by word processing systems enable telephone communication with typesetting equipment. This allows document files to be transmitted to telecommunicating typesetters, whereby high-quality text reproduction can be achieved. Many computer systems can achieve similar communication links; however, this is often a major technical problem on some systems, since the basic system design never intended computer-to-photocomposer communication.

3-13. Microcomputer-Based Word Processing

Small business and home computer systems

Microcomputers are being used by many small businesses and are even finding their way into many homes. Small business systems offer a variety of standard software packages, including payroll, general ledger, accounts payable, accounts receivable, inventory control, and (you guessed it) even word processing. Some of the microcomputer systems aimed at the personal computing or home market are also offering word processing software packages. Many of these microcomputer systems are available for well under $10,000 for the businessman and under

$3,000 for the home, including software and peripherals such as disk drives and low-cost printers.

Almost all the popular, small business computers have word processing (sometimes called "text-editing") packages. These software packages are frequently offered by the equipment manufacturers. Another source of word processing software is independent software companies that thrive on the sale of special-applications software systems. These companies often specialize in developing software packages compatible with computer equipment from specific manufacturers. If you own a small business system, you may want to look into the availability of word processing software from the manufacturer. If unavailable, don't give up; there may be another source.

Sources for word processing software

The functionality of microcomputer word processing software should be reviewed carefully. Some packages are quite good, while others leave much to be desired. Because some systems have limited memory and storage capacities, WP packages are often simple, line-oriented text editors that are not functionally competitive with large, special-purpose word processing systems. In addition, they are often designed by computer people for computer people instead of for word processing system operators. Documentation is often riddled with computer jargon, service is sometimes marginal or nonexistent, and, if the system's memory or storage is limited, functionality may be more of a nuisance than a help.

Check documentation and service

This is not to say that all small-system text editors are not good. There are some that may be exactly what you're looking for. It may be time well spent to investigate this market. Who knows, there may be a small system that is just right for your business problem.

3-14. THE MULTIFUNCTION INFORMATION SYSTEM

In the word processing field a multifunction information system is a word processing system that can perform many functions—hence, the term *multifunction* is used. However, there is no clear distinction between a word processor with many features and the so-called multifunction information system. Many word processing manufacturers use the term to identify their system as something special as compared to simple word processors that are restricted to performing only common text-editing functions. If a word processing system does everything that normal word processing systems do in addition to performing functions often restricted to general-purpose computer systems, then it qualifies as a multifunction information system. Multifunction systems often perform mathematical calculations; sort lists of names or numbers in alphabetical, numerical, and alphanumeric order; and communicate via telephone lines to other word processing or computer systems.

Performing a multitude of tasks

3-15. Administrative Support Systems

Administrative support systems are often multifunction word processing systems used in office areas in support of executives. These systems often have special features. These features allow executives to read incoming mail and to create, store, and review "tickler" files, appointment calendars, presentation materials, business performance information, and a host of other business-related documents on display screens located in their office. It is systems like these that have spawned the term *Office of the Future*. They not only support secretarial text editing, but also can be used to prepare, store, print, and distribute information contained in a company's central computer system data base. Teleconferencing is also a popular feature on administrative support systems. The teleconferencing feature usually allows two or more executives to review displayed documents simulta-

Special administrative features

neously and discuss them via telephone or office intercom.

The aim of administrative support systems is primarily executive productivity. The time of top company executives is precious. Therefore, any tool making their job easier and more efficient is valuable. Administrative support systems are thought of as such tools. Through these systems executives can quickly view company performance and financial information, improve communications with other company personnel, and take intelligent and prompt action in response to problems, thereby making better decisions and improving company performance. A typical administrative support system is illustrated in Figure 3-4.

Executive productivity the goal

3-16. The Merger of Word Processing and Data Processing

The technology used in modern word processing systems is actually an adaptation of that used in data processing (digital computer systems). From a technology standpoint, word processing and data processing have been merged since digital computer electronics was first applied to word processing in the late 1960s. In fact, a modern word processing system is a special-purpose digital computer system. A great deal of commonality exists in equipment, storage media, and terminology, and both word processing and data processing systems exist to process information.

WP, a special purpose DP system

However, there are major differences in the kinds of information handled and tasks normally performed, and operator background requirements differ largely. For example, data processing usually concentrates on performing tasks associated with payroll, accounts payable, accounts receivable, general ledger, and inventory control. Word processing concentrates

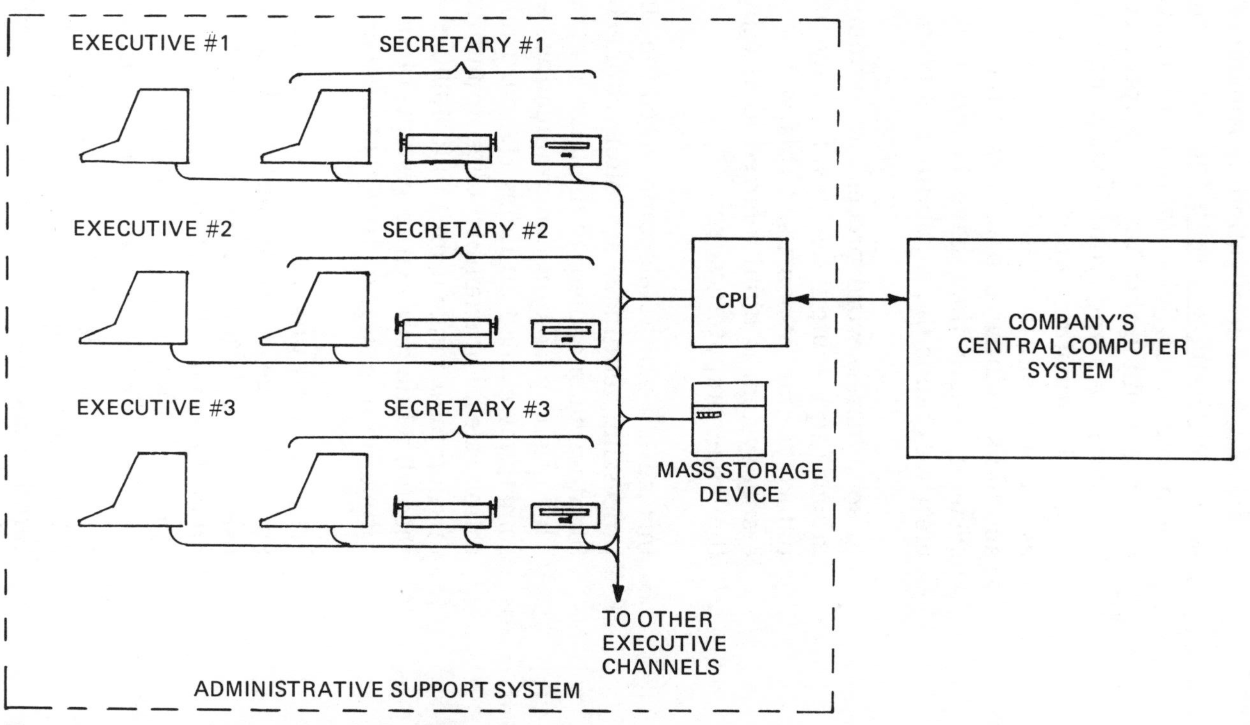

Figure 3-4. An Administrative Support System

on correspondence, product literature, administrative tables, lists, reports, and other information typically found in the office that is most often not complex enough for application of a business's powerful computer resources. With the advent of telephone communications (telecommunications) circuits and common communication forms (protocols) that allow computers and word processing systems to exchange information, word processing and data processing systems frequently take advantage of one another's peculiar capabilities. Combining the two systems where they have access to one another greatly expands the capabilities of both.

The work is the difference

In some cases, word processing systems act as terminals (input-output devices) for large, central computer systems. When used this way, a word processing system is often referred to as a *front end* for the large computer system.

Hard-wired is faster

Instead of using telecommunication links, word processing terminals are often connected directly (hard-wired or cabled) to the large computer system. This often speeds up communications at rates that sometimes exceed 30 times standard telecommunication rates. For example, telecommunication transmission rates range from 150 to 4,800 characters per second, while hard-wired systems often transmit information in excess of 10,000 characters per second.

Using WP terminals for DP input

When a word processing system is used as a front end for a large computer system, the word processor can input information, such as budget numbers or other financial information, directly from an administrative office area to the company's central computer system. Here the central computer, with its powerful "number crunching" capability, can perform complex mathematical computations and return the results directly to the office area printed on a letter-quality printer. Often, the results are stored locally on the word processor's storage media. The information can be reviewed, modified, and printed in view-graph (overhead projection) form for presentation in a meeting or printed in letter form for hard copy distribution. In addition, the computer system's mass storage media may be used to store word processing files. In this way local storage resources can be minimized.

These are only a few typical examples of the benefits that can be realized by merging DP and WP systems in support of business operations. Figure 3-5 contains a simplified diagram of a DP-WP system merger.

Merging DP and WP organizationally

In addition to merging WP and DP systems, there is a tendency for many businesses to merge DP and WP operations organizationally. Some have been successful while others have experienced problems. The key is to prepare people for change, ensure that the manager responsible is familiar with the personalities, functional responsibilities and problems, and user requirements of both areas. Almost invariably the DP manager assumes responsibility for the WP section in such an organizational merger. This is most common because DP managers usually have better technical background than WP managers. WP people are often apprehensive about being taken over by a DP manager, who may have little understanding of the pressures and service requirements common to WP operations. WP section supervision almost invariably requires excellent people-handling skills, since those working in the WP environment must cope with the pressure of deadlines on a daily (and sometimes hourly) basis. Not that this isn't true in the DP environment, but work in DP is generally more routine and easily planned. Computer people are logical by nature and avocation; WP people typically provide a quick-reaction service and must continually respond to unforeseen demands. As a manager, you should be certain that your WP supervisor has excellent people-handling skills. The supervisor should be someone people both like and respect.

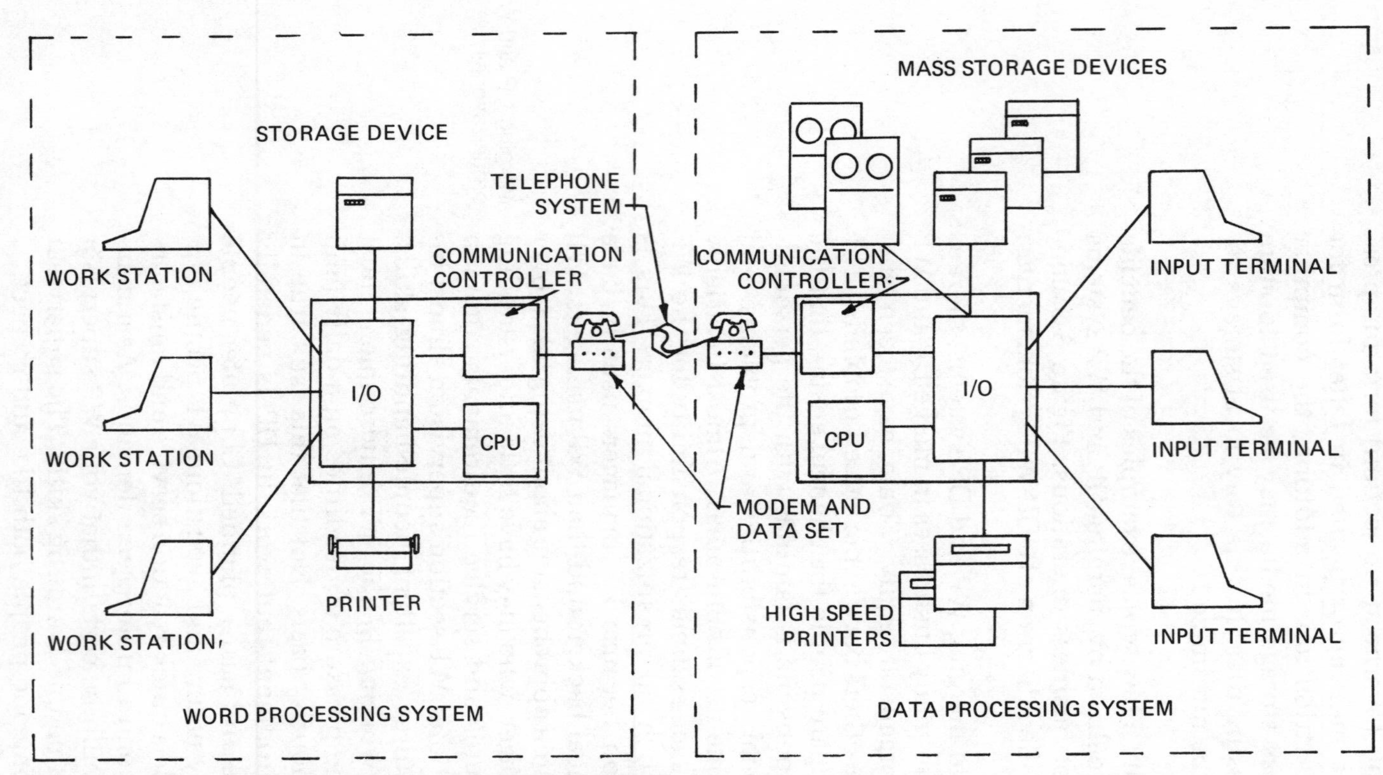

Figure 3-5. Data Processing–Word Processing System Merger

3-17. DICTATION SYSTEMS

Dictation systems, close kin to WP

Dictation systems can be categorized as word processing systems because they are used to process words. In addition, they are often used in conjunction with word processors. Some word processing system manufacturers are actually contemplating offering dictation equipment options on their word processing terminals. This could be a good idea, particularly for equipment used in word processing centers equipped with central dictation equipment. In Chapter 7, we'll look at dictation systems in some detail. Here, an overview of dictation systems is provided.

3-18. Types of Dictation Systems

Many kinds to choose from

Most people who have been kicking around in the business world for any length of time recognize that there has been a virtual explosion in the number and kinds of dictation equipment brought into the world. There are portable machines, desk-top machines, and even monstrously large machines that require an entire table or stand of their own. In addition to a variety of configurations, dictating systems use a variety of storage media. In the 1930s and '40s, wire machines existed. Reel machines, belt machines, cartridge machines, and even disk machines exist today. Within each of these types, many sizes, formats, and speeds exist. The proliferation of varieties of dictation equipment is a wonder; it can also be frustrating, particularly if your business has been around for a while and you try to standardize. You're going to find yourself throwing a lot of equipment away. You'll also find a number of people who "love" their particular machine, feel comfortable with it, and don't want to use anything else. But the biggest problem that faces most business managers is to get people to use dictation equipment at all. It is a painfully slow process to convert people away from handwritten copy to dictation. This problem is discussed in paragraph 7-3.

3-19. Dictation Equipment of the Future

There are a number of new technologies emerging in the area of speech synthesis and digital storage that will likely have a great impact on dictation equipment. For example, imagine a machine that has no moving parts and doesn't even use a magnetic medium to store recorded information. It might use a speech synthesis circuit which converts voice into digital computer data capable of being stored within a tiny magnetic-bubble memory device. The whole package could be smaller than the hand-held communicator used by Captain Kirk in "Star Trek." When you're ready for your secretary to type your dictation, she simply plugs the unit into her compact desk-top receptacle and begins transcribing. You pick up another speech input unit and are ready for another round of dictation. Since the units cost only around $29.95, you can have a number of units in supply.

An amazing breakthrough

If you happen to be out of town on business, you can telephone your dictation at high speed back to the office for transcription. For example, by using a telephone coupler unit, your speech input unit can transmit an hour's dictation to the office in a matter of seconds.

High speed dictation

Of course all this is futuristic, but some day not too far into the future we'll be seeing these kinds of transactions as commonplace. The technology and human creativity are all around us—it's only a matter of time.

3-20. WORD PROCESSING SYSTEM SOFTWARE

As a business manager, you shouldn't need to know all about word processing system or computer software. There are people who work for you, for your company, or for a service company that take care of these kinds of things. However, it may be helpful to understand some of the terminology to help you communicate with technical people. It should also be of value to know some of the relationships between software and word processing systems.

You should know

In the early days of electronics, almost everything was *hardware*. Nuts and bolts, wires, chassis, vacuum tubes, and all the electrical and electronic piece parts such as resistors, capacitors, and inductors were called hardware. The operation and maintenance manuals that described equipment operation and repair procedures at one time carried the name *software*. And software was indeed soft, paper being softer than steel, ceramic, and copper. So software is a term that has been in use for many years, and it didn't really begin with the data processing industry. But it is used more today than ever before, and it still applies to most things that aren't called hardware. If this makes sense to you, then you're in better shape than many who view these terms as mystical jargon used by technical people.

Software was soft

The field of digital electronics brought the computer and with the computer came more paper. This paper, in the form of punched cards and printer listings, was also called software. The punched cards carried coded information that either provided instructions to (programed) the computer or simply carried data (characters and numbers).

Later, new types of software evolved. These were different in configuration, but still performed the same job of inputting information to computers. The configurations that evolved included a variety of media, such as magnetic tapes, cards, and disks. Although punched cards are still used today, they are rapidly being replaced by magnetic media because magnetic media contain more information for their size and weight and are much easier to process, handle, and store.

New types of software

Today's computer and word processing system software, then, consists mostly of media used to input program instructions and data to the machines. In addition to media-resident program instructions and data, there are also electronic devices that contain program instructions and data. These devices, referred to as *firmware*, can be plugged into a computer or word processing system to modify program instructions. They are actually programable hardware, either programed at the factory or in the field. Some devices that qualify as firmware are called read-only memories (ROMS), programable read-only memories (PROMS), and electrically alterable, programable read-only memories (EAPROMS).

Firmware, a hybrid

3-21. Computer and Word Processing System Programs

Now that hardware, software, and firmware have been described, let's briefly look at what programs do.

Programs, a set of instructions

Programs are simply sets of instructions that control machine (word processing system) activities in response to specific operator commands. If the machine is to delete a text character in response to some predetermined sequence of operator keystrokes, it uses one set of program instructions. It uses another set of program instructions to insert a character. Hence, a computer program is fundamentally a compilation of instructions designed to perform certain tasks in response to operator actions. In some cases instructions are linked, or chained together. For a machine to accomplish a text move, it may require a half dozen sets of program instructions.

3-22. System-Resident and Media-Resident Software

Two kinds of common software systems

Some word processing systems are preprogramed at the factory by means of firmware and hardware. This is called *system-resident software*. Others use program instructions on media, such as disks, which are loaded into the system when it is turned on. This is called *media-resident software*. Most word processing systems use a combination of system-resident and media-resident software.

Word processing systems that use system-resident software tend to be faster than those using media-resident software. This is because the time required to search for and "fetch" an instruction from the media in response to an operator command is minimized. However, word processing systems that rely entirely on system-resident software are usually much less flexible than those using media-resident software. In fact, it often takes a field modification to change system features.

On the other hand, features of systems using media-resident software can be changed by simply inserting a new program medium, such as a program disk. When looking at systems, it may be important to determine how easy it is to add new system features. Some systems that rely on system-resident software are almost entirely inflexible. What you see is what you get. When they are upgradable, hardware modifications can be expensive and time-consuming. On a media-resident software system, the installation of a new program release that enables the system to perform additional or improved functions can be equally expensive. However, it may take only a matter of seconds to make the upgrade.

Changing system features made easy

If you decide to obtain a system that can be upgraded by simply changing the program medium, it's wise to check on software pricing. Some manufacturers sell or lease their systems and offer updated software at no charge. These often place almost all system functions on one program disk or cassette. Others, who rely heavily on the sale of software, charge high prices for program media that allow their system to perform various functions. These manufacturers often offer a library of program media.

Software marketed in different ways

3-23. Software Functionality

Since disks are the most common media used today on modern word processing systems, we'll use the term disk for media. It should be noted that word processing systems that use a variety of program disks to perform the machine's repertoire of functions are not as convenient from a user standpoint as those that use one program disk that supports all system functions. On a system that employs multiple-program disks, the operator must use a special sort disk to perform an alphabetical sort. If a mathematical calculation is required, a special math disk must be used. Changing disks takes time. The operator must find the desired disk, remove and store the previous one, insert the new one into the word processing system, and go through a loading sequence. When systems use one master program disk containing all system program instructions, the operator simply performs functions by entering a sequence of appropriate keystrokes.

Changing disks takes time

3-24. Software Reliability

Software reliability is a major concern among experienced word processing system users today. "How stable is the software?" is a very good question to ask. If it's a new system, or even an old one with a new software release, it's possible that you'll experience some system "bugs." This means that not all key sequences have been tested. When this happens, your operators will probably discover them. Since the word processing system hasn't been programed to handle the strange sequence, it may "crash." (*Crash* is a euphemism for die—the system simply freezes up and refuses to respond to any keyboard command.) When a system crashes, it must usually be turned off and then back on again. Crashes often result in the loss of documents. If the system crashes in the middle of a big rush job, it could be a disaster. Document recovery is sometimes possible, but not always. And recovery usually takes the help of a customer service representative who may be miles and hours away.

Verify software stability

Crashes can cause loss

The moral to this discussion is, Be sure that your system software is tried and true. New, untested software can be costly.

4-1. INTRODUCTION

This chapter describes some of the ways that word processing systems are applied in the day-to-day solution of business-related problems. It would take many volumes to describe all the ways that word processing systems are used, so only common applications are dealt with here. As you might imagine, new applications for word processing systems are being invented daily. As new word processing system configurations and features evolve, new applications are found. The whole process of new applications and new features is an interactive, self-stimulating one. New applications stimulate a round of ideas for added features; added features stimulate another round of ideas for new applications. As a business manager, you should seek to maintain an environment where creativity can flourish. You'll find that with the right atmosphere and tools, everyone in the organization can be a source of ideas for improved business performance.

How WP systems are used

Word Processing System Applications

4-2. SECRETARIAL SUPPORT

Almost everyone thinks of the secretary as the primary candidate for word processing systems. Indeed, secretaries were the first word processing system users. Secretaries type correspondence, type and maintain business records, transcribe dictation, and transmit information by mail, telephone, telex, or facsimile. There was a time when every secretary was considered a general secretary. Each did everything that came along. However, because secretaries began to specialize, they have been given more specific duties and corresponding titles. In some companies where secretaries have heavy keyboard duties, secretarial positions have been subdivided into administrative secretary, correspondence secretary, and in some cases, general secretary. They've recognized that secretaries who perform all the duties described above in addition to conducting telephone transactions, mail runs, document routing, hard copy file maintenance, and all the other activities that take them away from their work station are less effective as keyboard operators. When they are equipped with an expensive word processing system, this can be detrimental to the company's return on assets. To improve efficiency, correspondence secretaries were created to concentrate on keyboard-related secretarial duties.

Kinds of secretaries

A second advantage of having correspondence secretaries is that they usually become much more proficient in the use of their machine. Because they spend more time using their system, their learning curve is generally much steeper than that of administrative secretaries who only spend part of their time doing keyboard work. This proficiency normally results in substantial increases in keyboard productivity.

Dedicated WP personnel improves productivity

Improved cycle time is a third advantage of having dedicated correspondence secretaries. Whereas administrative secretaries must operate amidst interruptions such as answering phones and making reservations, correspondence secretaries' distractions are kept to the minimum. This lets them finish their jobs faster and usually permits improved concentration, resulting in better work quality.

4-3. ADMINISTRATIVE SUPPORT SYSTEMS

Administrative support systems were described in Chapter 3. In this chapter, some of the interactions between executives and the administrative support systems are described.

As mentioned in Chapter 3, an administrative support system is normally a special-purpose, multifunction word processing system. Many large companies have developed administrative support systems aimed at improving executive productivity and communications. In most cases, executives have terminals located in their office for direct access to the vast amount of information essential to effective business execution. They have access to special information such as the company's financial position, which is normally stored in the central computing system.

Direct access to information

One feature common to administrative support systems is that administrative secretaries also have terminals on their desks. This allows a secretary and her boss to view documents simultaneously. She can perform keyboard work as her boss dictates letters. Changes can be made as the document is developed. This is an improved form of communication between secretary and boss.

Another feature often offered by administrative support systems is calendar control. Executives with access to the system can maintain up-to-date calendars which are stored on the system. The executives can view both their own calendar and those of other executives. If one executive needs to schedule a meeting with another, he can review each of the calendars, select a time convenient to both, and enter it on both calendars.

Calendar feature helpful

The ability to view information on file in the company's central system is common. Some systems allow executives to display key business information, change certain financial indices, and view the results. This is sometimes called playing a *"what if"* game. The effects of increasing sales, reducing inventory, adjusting overhead, adding capital, increasing space, changing staffing levels, and other such manipulations lets executives see what effect such actions will have on the business. Cash flow, long-term debt service, and many other indices can be experimented with in this way, thereby making this feature invaluable in assisting executives with important business decisions.

Playing "what if"

4-4. TELECOMMUNICATIONS ON WORD PROCESSING SYSTEMS

Office communication systems have been in use for many years. Teletype and facsimile have been the mainstay of office communications for a long time. Facsimile began to replace teletype installations in the 1960s; now, facsimile is slowly giving way to word processing system-based telecommunications in many companies. Two advantages to facsimile are its relatively low cost and its ability to transmit line drawings and photographs. Some major drawbacks to facsimile include slow transmission speed, poor quality, and the necessity for operators to leave their work station to use a centralized facsimile machine. A facsimile transmission usually takes from one to three minutes per 8½-by-11-inch copy. The reproduction quality is normally faded or muddy-looking, because most facsimile machines use a line-scan reproduction technique that has fairly coarse resolution, that is, the lines are sometimes separated by white space. Word processing system telecommunication is presently limited to text. However, transmission speeds allow entire pages to be sent in a matter of seconds. Many systems allow operators at each work station to communicate without leaving their desks, thereby saving the time necessary to walk to a single machine used to support a large work area. The appearance of the received telecommunication

Fast transmission of correspondence

is letter-quality, because it is usually played out on the word processing system's letter-quality printer.

4-5. Telecommunications Uses

Businesses are discovering many valuable uses for telecommunications. Instead of hand-carrying or mailing correspondence, presentation material, or financial data, word processing systems are able to transmit this information in seconds. Airfare and postage savings often pay for the cost of telecommunications. Received telecommunication material can be captured on a local storage device, displayed on a screen for review, and revised before it is printed on paper. If appropriate, the revised document can be telecommunicated back to the point of origin so that the originators are aware of the changes.

Telecommunications sometimes less than postage

Another use for telecommunications is to link word processing systems to other devices which can compute, store, or output information in a more suitable manner. For example, telecommunication is commonly used to allow word processing systems to store information on large central computer systems or to transmit text files to photocomposition units for typesetting. These transactions are described in more detail later in this chapter.

Linking to other systems

4-6. Telecommunications Problems

When installing telecommunications on a word processing system, it is of primary importance to ensure that the language your system speaks is compatible with the language of those systems with which you wish to communicate. This language, sometimes called *protocol,* is simply a data code used to represent specific characters, numbers, punctuation marks, symbols, and spaces. Aside from protocol, there are other considerations. These include electrical levels, speed, physical connections, and synchronization compatibility of communication signals. For example, if you have a system equipped with an acoustic coupler that uses 300-baud 2741 protocol, there's no way you're going to talk to one that uses a 2400-baud 201C modem and 3780 bisynchronous communications. Had enough? Many have.

They must speak the same language

As a business manager, you shouldn't have to be concerned with communications nomenclatures, electrical levels, protocols, and couplers and modems. You should insist that those people representing word processing, data processing, photocomposition, and whatever else is involved provide you with a complete system integration plan. As a minimum the plan should include

Assure communications compatibility

1. Complete communication specifications of all systems involved
2. A diagram and list of all required equipment and cables, specifying connector types, cable lengths, and costs
3. A list of all software modifications required to achieve specified communications
4. A system integration schedule showing actions, times, and responsibilities, including installation, interconnection, testing, and operator training
5. A money-back guarantee that those functional communication features specified by you will work.

4-7. Communication Configurations

Before leaving our discussion about telecommunications, it may be valuable to look at typical ways that word processing systems are connected for communications. Acoustic couplers and modems were mentioned in paragraph 4-6. Both of these devices, which have been used for years in the data processing field, link work processing systems to the telephone system, allowing communications to be sent and received over telephone lines.

4-8. Acoustic Couplers, Modems, and Hard Wiring. An acoustic coupler, shown in Figure 4-1, is equipped with a telephone handset cradle. The cradle, which is essentially two rubber cups (one for the mouthpiece and the other for the earphone), allows coupling of a signal from the word processing system's communications circuit to the telephone system. A modem, derived from the term modulate-demodulate, connects the word processing system's communications circuit to the telephone system by means of direct, hard-wire interface. A modem is shown in Figure 4-2. Both acoustic couplers and modems first convert data signals generated by a word processing system to a level and form suitable for telephone transmission and then couple those signals to the phone system. Modems are capable of faster communication speeds and have less noise problems than acoustic couplers. They also eliminate the need to press the telephone handset physically into the coupler's cradle prior to sending or receiving communications. Both acoustic couplers and mo-

Converting computer data to sound

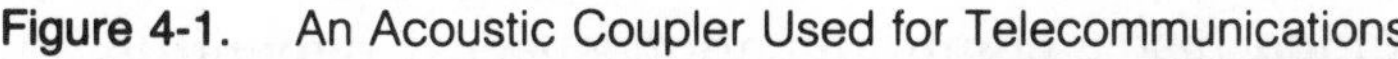

Figure 4-1. An Acoustic Coupler Used for Telecommunications

Figure 4-2. A Modem Used for Telecommunications

dems may be purchased; however, they are commonly leased.

A third method of communication connection is by means of direct cable, often called hard wire. This method can be used to connect one word processing system to another or to some other device such as a data processing system or photocomposer. The communications circuits that interface the two devices must be compatible. Hard wiring often results in much faster communication speeds, depending on the capability of the communication controller circuits of each device.

Hard wire the fastest

4-9. Telecommunications Access. With some background as to how word processing systems are connected to the telephone line or hard-wired to other devices, we'll now take a look at some typical ways systems are configured to achieve communications.

Some multiple–work station word processing systems equipped for telecommunications can accomplish communications from any work station on the system. Figure 4-3 shows such a system. A system that allows communication from any work station normally is equipped with a communications controller circuit located in the central processing unit (CPU) of the system. In addition, the communication port (connector) is located at the CPU. As a file is communicated on this type of system, the controlling work station can return to standard text editing and begin creating a new document or edit an old one. This concurrent communications process is called *background communications*. The work station can be used for text editing in foreground while the communication transaction is being executed in background. These systems also receive communications in background, while the work stations are text-editing in foreground. Incoming communications are automatically filed on the systems' storage media. When system operators wish to view received communications, they simply display the file that contains the incoming traffic. Often, systems that contain background communications capability display a message on the screen to let system operators know that correspondence has been received.

System connections

Concurrent communications and editing

Some systems use only one work station for communications. When this is the case, the system's communications controller circuits and port are located at the communicating work station. Figure 4-4 shows

Figure 4-3. Telecommunications from Multiple Work Stations on a Word Processing System

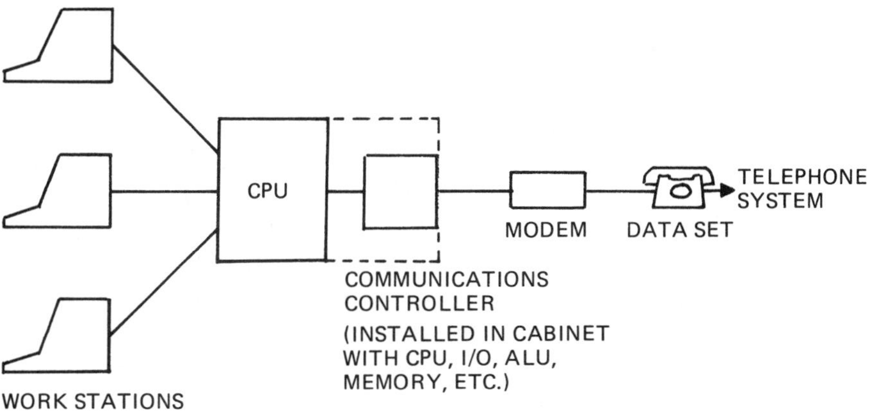

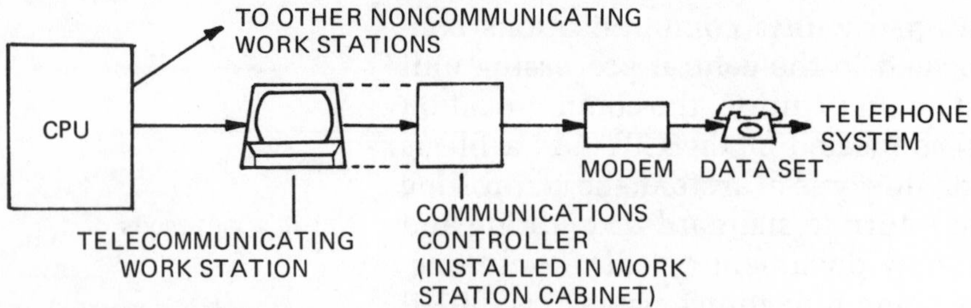

Figure 4-4. A Single Telecommunications Work Station on a Word Processing System

One communicating workstation

this kind of system. When a communication transaction is required, the operator usually displays the file on the screen, telephones the receiving word processing system to notify the attendant operator, and transmits the file in foreground. This means that when the work station is being used for communication, it can't be used for text creation or editing.

4-10. Autocall, Autoanswer, and Manual Call. The background system described in paragraph 4-9 sent and received messages without mention of dialing the receiving word processing system. This is not always the case. Many systems equipped with background communications must still telephone the receiving word processing system. When this is done, it is a manual call operation. However, many systems are equipped with *autocall, autoanswer,* and *autodial* features. The machines involved conduct the entire communications transaction themselves, including dialing, answering, and terminating the transmission when complete.

Communications can be automatic or manual

Frequently, word processing systems feature communication menus that are used to guide, or *prompt,* operators through the communication routine. These menus lead them through document selection and addressing and provide a list of system telephone numbers to choose from. Once the operator selects the receiving system, the appropriate key strokes are made, and the message is on its way. These systems

Communication menus

usually allow transmission of a document to one or more recipients in one transaction.

As can be seen, telecommunications has become a sophisticated discipline. When considering communications, it's necessary that you know what you're getting into. Know what you need, explain your requirements carefully to those responsible for supplying you with your equipment, and ensure that compatibility exists between all equipment and systems, the telephone company, and the business you're trying to support.

Know what you need

4-11. WORD PROCESSING CENTERS

Before getting into a detailed discussion of word processing equipment in word processing centers, it should be valuable to understand some ways that word processing centers are structured to support business operations. Word processing centers vary widely in services offered, size of the operation they support, and how they are administrated. Our discussion will address three variations in word processing center organization:

Types of WP organization

1. Large, consolidated word processing centers
2. Large centers with satellite operations
3. Decentralized satellite centers

4-12. Large, Consolidated Word Processing Centers

With the advent of relatively expensive word processing equipment, some business managers felt it would be good to concentrate their WP equipment in a production environment where it could be used more efficiently. Often secretaries and clerical personnel were moved from jobs where they were in direct support of administrative and professional personnel to new jobs in word processing centers. A diagram of a typical word processing center is

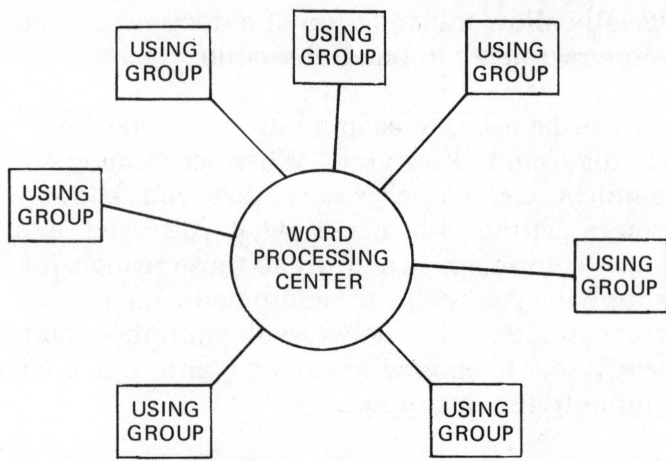

Figure 4-5. A Typical Word Processing Center, Simplified Diagram

shown in Figure 4-5. Some word processing centers began to look like manufacturing operations. Sophisticated production control systems were developed, work input and output was carefully measured, and some centers began operating on two and three shifts. Needless to say, the emphasis on production and productivity measurement systems resulted in increased keyboard productivity. Also, new career paths opened up for keyboard operators. With the new paths came opportunities for promotion to supervisory and group leadership positions. However, undesirable things also resulted. These included

A production environment

1. A feeling of dehumanization on the part of those transferred from a quiet office environment into centers that sometimes resembled "sweatshops"
2. Resentment on the part of adminstrative and professional personnel who suffered loss of personalized secretarial support
3. A lack of commitment on the part of center personnel toward specific company programs and users

Undesirable results from central operations

4. A lack of confidence by users in the center's willingness to respond to their needs
5. Increased keyboard operator turnover due to shift work.

Because of the problems outlined above, many centers failed. The trend was to return to the way it was before the advent of central word processing.

Some well-planned centers work successfully. In fact, many are in existence today. The difference is that the planning considered all the people involved in the move toward centralization—it included both center personnel and users. If you are inclined to centralize, it may be wise to think through a transition that points up the advantages to all the people involved, assigns specific word processing personnel in support of certain users or groups of users, and ensures that users still have administrative as well as keyboard support.

Some work quite well

4-13. Large Word Processing Centers Supplemented by Satellite Operations

Figure 4-6 contains a diagram of a large word processing center augmented by satellite centers. By distributing some of the workload from the central word processing center to satellite word processing centers, closer contact with users can be maintained. Sometimes satellites are created on an organizational basis, while others are positioned geographically. In either case, users identify with satellite personnel and generally feel that their support is more personalized.

Satellites often establish personalized service

In addition to structuring work by area, sometimes satellite centers concentrate on processing quick-turnaround jobs. Larger, more complex jobs are usu-

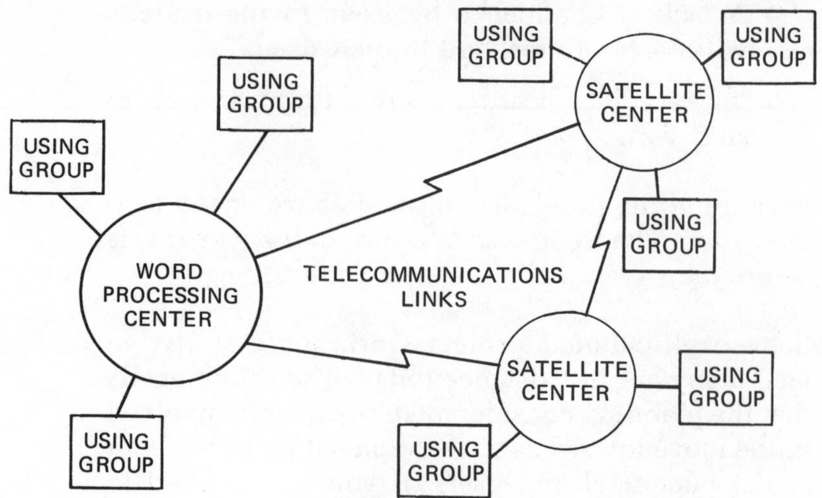

Figure 4-6. A Large Word Processing Center Supplemented by Satellite Word Processing Centers

ally sent to the business's bigger central word processing center. Here, more specialized equipment can handle mathematical equations that use special symbols, prepare material for typesetter or photocomposer input, or add illustrations and photographs. Because large, complex jobs involve more reviews, longer schedules, and a greater number of people, equipment, and process steps, greater production control and coordination effort are required.

Work allocation

One major advantage in having satellite centers is to prevent quick-reaction jobs from interfering with more complex, long-term projects. When the same center, people, and equipment must be used to process both quick-turnaround "rush" jobs and long-term projects, the production process becomes quite inefficient. People find themselves being pulled off one job to work on another. They are continually stopping and starting. The time required to stop and start, the loss of momentum, and the possibility of a job's "falling through the crack" or being lost entirely results in a high-cost, low-yield operation.

Isolate quick turnaround from long-term production

Another problem associated with mixing work in a single center is that the administrative controls necessary to cope with large, complex jobs is significantly greater than the controls needed for a quick-reaction job that takes only an hour or two. The tendency is to develop a single production control system for a center. This results in having small job users pay the same price for production control as large job users. Figure 4-7 contains an example of a production control record. The information is probably valid for a fifty-page report. It's a costly burden for a two-page letter.

Avoid administrative overhead

Before leaving our discussion of satellite and central word processing centers, one more benefit should be mentioned. By having satellite centers, more opportunity for the promotion of word processing personnel exists. Each satellite requires a lead person in addition to the supervisory personnel in the central facility. People who demonstrate their ability to supervise in the satellites make natural candidates for more responsibility in the large center. This is an excellent benefit to the business, and it offers career incentive to word processing personnel.

Opportunity for promotion

4-14. Decentralized Satellite Centers

Figure 4-8 shows a group of decentralized satellite word processing centers. Here, clusters of word processing equipment are set up to support the keyboard requirements of surrounding business operations. There is really very little difference between a business that uses satellites and one that uses a central word processing facility. The primary difference is that small, meagerly equipped satellites are sometimes expected to process documents beyond their equipment capability. When this happens—for example, when jobs requiring typesetting or artwork

Know your limitations and identify alternatives

PUBLICATIONS SCHEDULE AND PRODUCTION RECORD

DATE PREPARED	ORIGINATOR	EXT	EDITOR	CHARGE NO.	JOB/PART NO.

SUBJECT OR TITLE

SECURITY CLASSIFICATION	GROUP NO.	SPECIFICATIONS	
☐ U ☐ C ☐ S ☐ SA ☐ CO.CLASS.			☐ REQUESTED ☐ CONTRACTUAL

SCOPE OF WORK

INVENTORY	NEW	REV	PICK UP
M/S PAGES TEXT			
M/S PAGES TABLES			
ART			
PHOTOS			
OTHER			
TOTAL			

DATA PRODUCTION

FORMAT
- ☐ CORPORATE
- ☐ DIV. A
- ☐ DIV. B
- ☐ REPORT/PROPOSAL
- ☐ MIL- SPEC (ABOVE)
- ☐ ______

TEXT LIMITS
- ☐ 6.5 X 9
- ☐ ______

TYPE STYLE
- ☐ MTSC
- ☐ PHOTOCOMP.
- ☐ ______

PAGINATE FOR PRINTING
- ☐ ONE SIDE ONLY
- ☐ BACKED- UP

REPRO STOCK
- ☐ BUG
- ☐ CORP. PLAIN
- ☐ DIV. A
- ☐ DIV. B
- ☐ PLAIN
- ☐ BOND
- ☐ ______

REPRODUCTION

☐ TOTAL NUMBER PAGES ☐ TOTAL PRINTED COPIES

- ☐ 50 LB.
- ☐ 60 LB.
- ☐ PEARL
- ☐ ONE SIDE
- ☐ BACK UP
- ☐ STD COVER
- ☐ SPECIAL COVER
- ☐ OTHER ______ (SEE REMARKS)

- ☐ COLLATE
- ☐ CERLOX BIND
- ☐ 3-HOLE PUNCH
- ☐ POST BIND
- ☐ ACCO BIND
- ☐ CORNER STAPLE
- ☐ SIDE STITCH
- ☐ TAPE
- ☐ SADDLE STITCH
- ☐ ______

ACTUAL REPRO PAGES PRODUCED	
TEXT	
ART	
TEXT/ART	
PHOTOS	
TOTAL PAGES	

ACTUAL NO. COPIES PRODUCED

BOUND	UNBOUND	VELLUM	NEGS

COPIES RECIEVED

NO. COPIES	SIGNATURE	DATE

REMARKS

______

SCHEDULED DATES

MANUSCRIPT TO TECH EDIT		MANUSCRIPT TO PRODUCTION		ART TO PRODUCTJON		RC/RPO-ART TO 1st REVIEW	RC/RPO-ART 1st REVIEW COMPLETE	RC/RPO-ART CHANGES COMPLETE	ART/PMT'S PASTE-UP	TO FINAL REVIEW	REPRO TO PRINTING	PRINT & BIND COMPLETE
START	CUTOFF	START	CUTOFF	START	CUTOFF							

REVISED DATES

ACTUAL DATES

Figure 4-7. Typical Production-Control Record

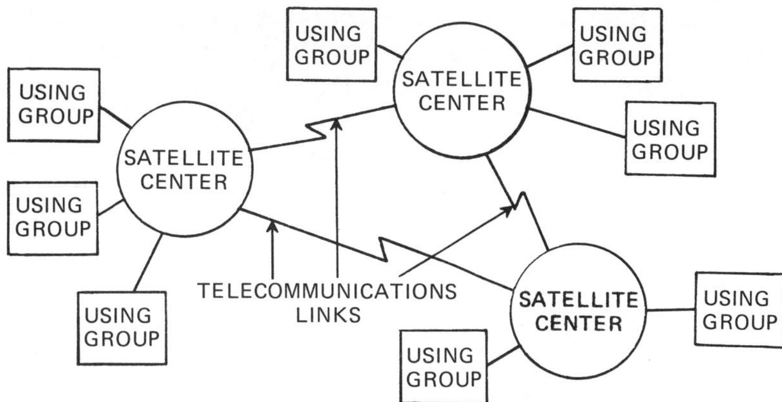

Figure 4-8. Satellite Word Processing Centers

are received—it is usually necessary to turn to outside agencies or publication vendors.

4-15. Word Processing Center Equipment

You'll find just about every type and brand of equipment imaginable in word processing centers. Some centers are not much more than "typing pools" (a term normally distasteful to word processing system operators). With the advent of display-based communicating systems, central dictation systems, and a number of new peripheral devices, word processing centers are becoming areas packed with new electronic marvels. Peripherals include such things as communication devices, printing devices, large mass-storage devices, optical character readers capable of scanning printed text and inputting it to the system, and other equipment attached to and used with word processing and data processing systems.

WP centers becoming packed with electronic marvels

Large, sophisticated central word processing centers are often supported by several satellite centers. Modern telecommunications equipment allows satellite centers to send and receive documents to and from the central system. In addition, the central system can often communicate with the business's central DP computer system. When the central word processing center is equipped with a photocomposer, files resident to the business's DP system can be pulled down to the central word processing center, formatted for typesetting, and prepared on a photocomposer in a form and quality suitable for publication.

WP centers can merge DP to photocomposition

Photocomposition will be addressed later in this chapter. It is mentioned here to demonstrate what can be achieved in a well-organized business that is equipped with modern word processing equipment.

4-16. OTHER USES FOR WORD PROCESSING TERMINALS

The concept of using word processing system work stations as input terminals for other systems was mentioned in paragraphs 3-13 and 4-15. The next three paragraphs will describe how word processing work stations can be used as terminals in support of

1. Financial reporting
2. Record storage and retrieval
3. Photocomposition.

4-17. Financial Reporting

Every business of any size stores profit-and-loss information, data on accounts payable and receivable, asset inventory data, financial models, economic analysis and trending information, and a myriad of other financial information necessary to plan and execute business operations and to measure business performance. Before the advent of the digital computer system, financial information was processed by hand. This limited companies from developing sophisticated financial reporting systems and to some extent forced business administrators to manage "by the seat of their pants." Today, computer systems allow businesses to rapidly store and retrieve huge masses of financial information. A busi-

Information exploitation vital to decisions

ness's ability to exploit financial information is key to its success. The exploitation of this information is considered vital to intelligent decision making by many business managers.

Many companies use centralized computer systems to store, compute, reformat, and output financial information. The need to input and output new or changed information in the administrator's office area has been met for many years by placing DP terminal equipment, such as keyboard devices and printers, in the office. As word processing equipment arrived on the scene, the office started to fill up with DP terminals, facsimile and teletype equipment, copiers, and word processing systems. Not only did all this equipment begin to gobble up valuable space, but the area also became a maze of wires and noisy machines. Secretarial and clerical personnel required substantial training in order to use all the different kinds of equipment.

An equipment explosion

As if this weren't enough, it seemed like something was always breaking. The cost of equipment, leases, and maintenance contracts was getting astronomical. Equipment maintenance people and marketing representatives seemed to be in the office on a round-the-clock basis. If they weren't fixing something, they were trying to sell something. If they weren't selling something, they were just making a courtesy call, which consisted primarily of dropping by to shoot the bull.

The modern word processing system and its ability to act as a computer input-output terminal has solved many of these problems. The machine can call up computer-stored information files, input changes, allow the central computer to perform necessary computations, and output the resulting information on a letter-quality printer. The quality of both input and output has enhanced the readability of the information as well as its appearance. If the information must be prepared for a meeting, it can be refor-

Modern WP a strong tool

matted locally and printed in a large, easy-to-read type size suitable for overhead projection.

Special word processing features, such as the double underscore and the decimal tab which aligns numbers on decimal points, help improve the ease of financial data preparation. The word processing system's ability to double as a computer input-output terminal has eliminated DP terminal equipment. Its ability to telecommunicate correspondence has in some cases eliminated facsimile and teletype equipment. Its ability to print multiple copies has reduced the need for copier equipment. Its ability to store administrative information has reduced file space. All of these are space-saving benefits. Other benefits include reduced training and service requirements, easier access to vital financial information, and improved report quality and visibility. All are considered important by most business managers.

One system does more

4-18. Record Storage and Retrieval

Record storage and retrieval, whether financial, personnel-related, legal, or simply historical, represent a rather cumbersome and sometimes expensive proposition. Document retention is cumbersome because people save things for reasons which are often based on emotion rather than policy. Storage areas fill up rapidly, and more storage space must be found. Drawers grow into file cabinets, file cabinets grow into closets, closets into rooms, and rooms into warehouses. Then comes the problem of retrieval. Just try and find something where vague categories and haphazard records exist. It's even harder when no records are kept.

Buried in paper

When a business establishes a well-thought-out retention plan for company documentation, it's on its way to improving retention efficiency. People know what to save and what to throw away. They know where to put things, how to record their location, and how to find them when they are needed. They also know when they can purge file space. This in itself can save the company money.

With the application of word processing systems to file retention, what at one time was kept on paper in office file cabinets is now placed on magnetic storage media for local use. A typical single-sided, ten-inch flexible magnetic disk, which is commonly used by word processing systems, can store from 60 to 120 standard pages of text. This process is often referred to as *archiving* a document to "floppy disk." When appropriate, the word processing system can telecommunicate stored documents to a mass-storage device connected to the company's central computer system. This purges local archive disks so they can be reused.

Storing files on media

Many companies are using micrographics equipment which allows hard-copy records to be photographed and placed on microfilm or microfiche. Another type of micrographics equipment, called computer output microfilm (COM), works in conjunction with computer systems. COM systems are used to convert computer-stored information to microfilm or microfiche. When copies are required, blow-back equipment is used to enlarge and project the microfilm image onto photosensitive paper.

The use of micrographics

Another benefit of having documents filed on microfilm is a company's ability to distribute relatively large amounts of information on small pieces of film. For example, a thousand-page document can be mailed in a standard envelope if it is reduced to microfiche.

We've looked at two methods of word processing system storage and retrieval. One method used local archive storage media. The second used telecommunications to remote mass-storage devices capable of retaining millions of characters. The intelligent use of micrographics equipment has also been key

Establish a retention plan

to efficient record retention. Regardless of the system used, the first step is to establish a retention plan that spells out what is to be stored, where it is to be stored, how it is to be stored, and when it can be destroyed.

4-19. Photocomposition

Photocomposition replaced hot type

The presence of photocomposers, which are used to set publication-quality type on photosensitive paper, is being felt by the in-house publishing market. When typesetting used "hot type" equipment, it required operators with specialized skills. It was common for typesetters to endure long apprenticeship programs before reaching the journeyman stage. With the advent of electronic *photo*composition equipment, productivity and operator proficiency rocketed.

Many common features

Photocomposition equipment, like word processing equipment, has become increasingly sophisticated over the last decade. Many common elements between photocomposition and word processing equipment are evolving. Display-based photocomposers with many of the same text-editing features offered by word processing system text editors are being offered by almost all large manufacturers. Photocomposers still use a lot of hot-type terminology, but with some training a good word processing operator can adapt quickly to photocomposer operation. Operators must, however, learn typesetting terminology in order to understand and control type size, line lengths, spacing, etc. In addition, photocomposer operators must be familiar with a set of commands that must be imbedded in text. These commands serve as instructions to the photocomposer for format and type-style control.

A different set of terms

Although most photocomposers have their own keyboards, some are simply output devices. These are either cable-connected to word processing terminals or equipped to read tape or disk media prepared on compatible work stations. Even photocomposers that have their own keyboards can frequently use media

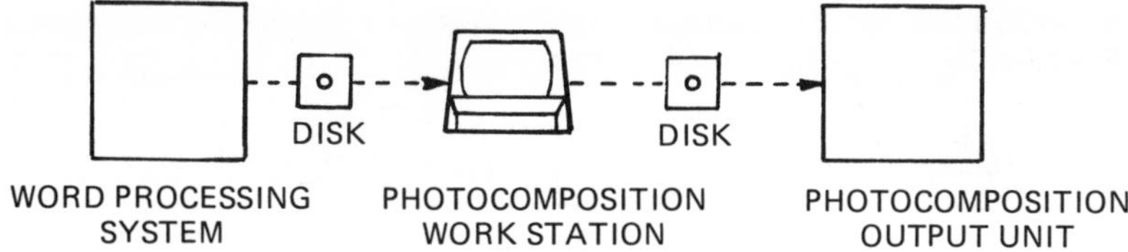

Figure 4-9. Word Processing System to Photocomposition System Interface through Diskette Transfer

prepared by word processing work stations. Some word processing system vendors offer photocomposers that are fully compatible. Compatibility can mean several things, depending on circumstances:

1. The medium, most often floppy disk, can be prepared on a word processor and read by a photocomposer.
2. The word processing system is hard wire–connected to the photocomposer, which is simply a system output device.
3. The photocomposer is equipped with telecommunications and can receive compatible telecommunications transmitted by a word processing system.
4. The photocomposer is equipped with a special "black box" that can translate a disk prepared on a word processing system to one that can be read by the photocomposer.

Compatibility advantages

Figures 4-9 through 4-11 show some typical word processing system-to-photocomposition equipment interconnections.

Figure 4-10. Word Processing System to Photocomposition System Interface through Hard Wire Interconnection

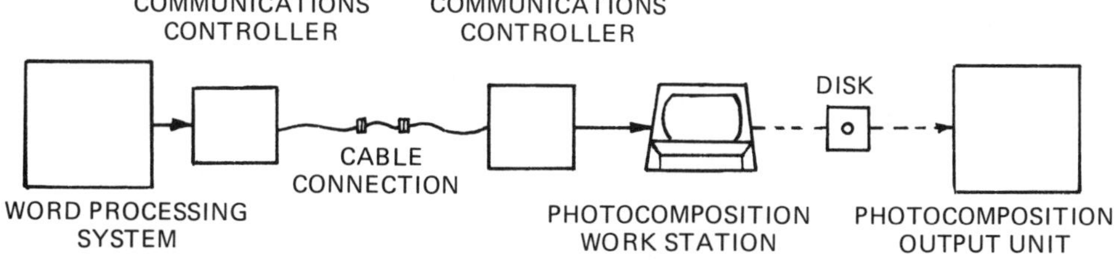

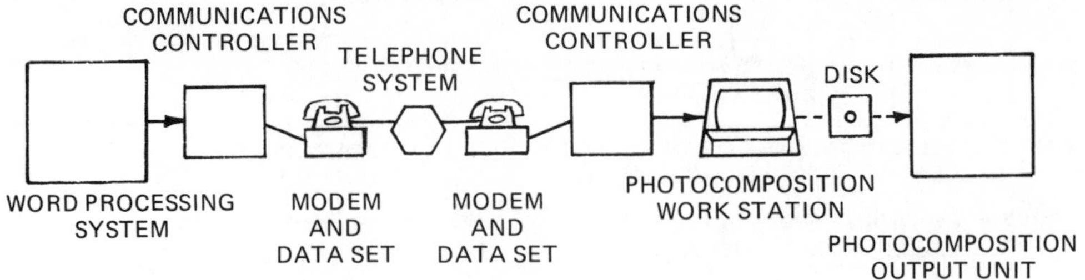

Figure 4-11. Word Processing System to Photocomposition System Interface through Telecommunications

4-20. APPLICATIONS SUMMARY

Some word processing requirements and corresponding features common to many businesses are described in this section. Again, it is impossible to describe all the ways that features can be applied to solving problems. However, just knowing a few general capabilities will let you apply the same approaches to solving problems in your operation.

4-21. Keyboard Entry Power

Faster input speed

It has been said that electronic typing systems are approximately twice as productive as standard typewriters, where display-based word processing systems are from four to five times more productive.

In this section, a description of keyboard entry power will be discussed. Keyboard power really addresses those features offered by most display-based word processing systems that allow operators to be more productive as they enter text from their work station. These include

Keyboard advantages

1. Automatic return
2. Automatic format control
3. Text-editing features
4. File support
5. Concurrent input-output.

4-22. Automatic Return. Automatic return allows an operator to enter text without being concerned about the return key used on conventional typewriters. The system simply takes the last word typed on a line and automatically "wraps" it around to the beginning of the next line if it is too long. If not, the word remains at the end of the last line typed and the cursor, which is a small square or bar of light showing the operator where text is being entered, automatically moves to the beginning of the next line to be typed. In addition to ignoring the return key, the automatic return feature lets the operator concentrate on the copy being typed without watching or listening for line endings. Some system manufacturers claim between two and five percent increase in typing speed through automatic line return.

Automatic word wrap

4-23. Automatic Format Control. By being able to adjust margins, line spacing, right-hand justification, centering, automatic indent, decimal tabs, and other features, the keyboard operator can make major format adjustments prior to text entry and then do free-form text entry. Another approach used is to do free-form text entry and then arrange the document using system format control once the keyboard entry work is complete. In either case, the operator doesn't have to agonize over format changes. By displaying the document and making a few keystrokes, the format can be adjusted prior to playout without a significant amount of effort.

Free-form typing makes it easier

4-24. Text-Editing Features. Text-editing features such as strikeover, insert, delete, move, copy, search, and replace are valuable to keyboard entry power. One of the barriers to speed on conventional typewriters is the fear of making errors. Operators tend to be very cautious. They know that corrections can be time-consuming. A correction means stopping, backspacing, and retyping, using correction fluid, rolling the page and erasing, or performing some other operation that takes from several seconds to perhaps a minute.

Removing a barrier to speed

Text-editing features free operators from the fear of making keyboard errors. When they detect a mistake, they simply backspace and keyboard in the correction. If they omit a word, they simply insert it; the text is automatically shifted by the system to accommodate the insert. If they enter unnecessary characters or words, they simply delete them. Once again, the system automatically shifts text to accommodate the deletion. If they wish to move material, they simply identify it and relocate it with a few keystrokes. Text-editing features are probably the single most significant factor in increased keyboard speed. An operator's keyboard speed can increase as much as twenty-five percent thanks to a word processing system's text-editing features.

Changes are quick and easy

4-25. File Support. Word processing systems have file management systems that allow system users to file documents on the system's media, label them, and retrieve them when needed. An important characteristic of a good word processing system is the ease of filing and retrieving documents. Most systems allow operators to name their documents on a file index. Some allow the operator to assign a document number for identification and retrieval purposes, while other systems automatically assign system-generated numbers. Some systems display the date the document was last filed and the number of pages in the file index. There are even some that list the number of keystrokes and the time spent creating the document. This kind of information can be quite valuable when making productivity studies.

Document location a snap

There are systems that have extremely weak file management systems. Operators must often create a separate filing document which lists all text documents and their locations on the storage media. These systems are in the minority; however, when looking for productive word processing systems, it is important to investigate the quality of the file management system used.

File management should be carefully reviewed

4-26. Concurrent Input-Output. The ability of a word processor to print documents while another is being entered or edited is significant. This feature is often called concurrent or simultaneous printing. Many systems allow operators to queue up several documents to be printed at a time. Once the printing command is started, the operator can simply begin working on new material while the printer prepares the queued documents. Continuous-form paper and forms tractors, which automatically advance the paper, eliminate the need for the operator to sheet-feed a printer as each page is completed. The combination of concurrent input-output and automatic paper feed is valued in many businesses.

Print while typing

4-27. Some Common Word Processing Problems

You'll see a detailed description of most of the features offered by word processing systems in Chapters 5 and 9. Here, we'll discuss a half dozen typical business problems in which word processing systems have been extremely helpful:

1. Iterative documents
2. Form letters
3. Tabular material
4. Multiple-format documents
5. Reformatted documents
6. Financial documents.

Typical business applications

4-28. Iterative Documents. Iterative (sometimes called "multiple-pass") documents are those that are subject to two or more passes through the typewriter. For example, the document is typed, handed to the originator for review, and retyped with changes. Documents that have many reviewers often pass through the typewriter many times. This is particularly true

Iterative documents are easier

of merchandising copy such as brochures or product data sheets. When using a typewriter, the document is normally rekeyboarded with each pass. Of course, there are times when correction fluid or "cut-and-paste" processes are used. Even these are time-consuming.

There are significant advantages in using a word processing system over a typewriter. These are

WP savings

1. Less keyboarding time—only the changed areas must be retyped.
2. Higher-quality output—letter-perfect typed output instead of correction fluid or cut-and-paste.
3. Improved originator productivity—the originators must verify only the changed areas for accuracy; the possibility for typographical errors to creep in during a retype cycle is eliminated.
4. Faster turnaround—once changes are typed, the document can be played out on a high-speed printer device.

4-29. Form Letters. Before word processing systems, form letters were often typed one at a time or preprinted with variable information, such as names and addresses, typed in separately. With a modern word processing system, form letters can be keyboarded and stored on the system. When they are needed, the operator simply displays the form letter on the screen, types in the variable information, and prints a copy. Many systems offer a merge feature which allows a list of variables to be prepared and merged with the body, sometimes called the mask, of the form letter. The system automatically inserts the variable information at the locations specified in the body of the form letter. Word processing system advantages include

Form letters a snap

1. Less keyboarding time—only variables must be typed.

2. Higher-quality output—every copy is letter-perfect.

3. More attractive output—proper spacing is achieved automatically, whereas preformatted form letters often have too much white space around short variables and not enough room for long variables.

WP savings

4. Faster turnaround—form letters can be played out on a high-speed printer device.

4-30. Tabular Material. Alignment of tabular material on typewriters often takes a lot of planning and counting. Centering material under column headings and counting the letters in words to be certain they fit in a column before they are typed are just two of the things that can be time-consuming on a typewriter. Corrections can be nightmares. An entire table may have to be redone to accommodate the insertion or deletion of even a single table entry.

Alignment made easy

Word processing systems permit automatic centering, eliminating the need for character counting. With a display-based word processing system, table entries may be experimented with on the screen. If they don't fit, they can be deleted or moved. Standard text-editing features make tabular typing much easier on word processing systems. Advantages include

1. Less keyboarding time—automatic centering and tab features eliminate the need for excessive calculations; trial placement can be performed on a display screen and adjusted to fit with text-editing features; column headings can be moved from page to page through a system copy feature to eliminate retyping of identical text.

WP savings

2. Higher-quality output—tabular material can be inspected and adjusted on the display screen to ensure that it is well-balanced before final playout.

3. Faster turnaround—tabular material can be made up in less than half the time it takes on a standard typewriter; the benefits attributed to iterative documents also apply when changes are required.

4-31. Multiple-Format Documents. Multiple-format documents are those that require changes in margins, in line spacing, and in type style within the document. All can be very time-consuming with a standard typewriter. For example, if margins change, the typist must calculate both the left- and right-hand margins and calculate new centering. If indented material is to be justified on the right, every line must be counted and hand-adjusted. Changes in type style mean changing the type element each time italics or some other style is called for.

Different formats no problem

Most word processing systems offer features that allow operators to adjust formats throughout the text. Automatic right-hand justification, automatic centering, and changes in line spacing and margins can be done with a few simple keystrokes. Changes in style can be accomplished through the use of stop codes. These are operator commands which tell the system to stop printing to allow the operator to make a type-font change. Once the printer completes typing of the new style print, another stop code is used to go back to the original type style.

Changing type style

Some systems use dual-head printers that can be loaded with two type styles at a time. The operator can call for style one or style two as the text is created. This eliminates completely the need for stops and changes. Of course, to justify the cost of a dual-head printer over that of a single-head printer requires that there be a significant demand for multiple-style typing.

Some of the advantages offered by a word processing system for multiple-format document preparation include

1. Less keyboarding time—automatic centering and margin-change features eliminate the need for excessive calculations.
2. Higher-quality output—reformatted material can be inspected and adjusted on the display screen to ensure accurate arrangement before final playout.
3. No type-style changes—systems supporting dual-head printers eliminate the need to change type fonts.
4. Faster turnaround—material can be reformatted "on the fly"; the benefits attributed to iterative documents also apply when changes are required.

WP savings

4-32. Reformatted Documents. Reformatted documents are those in which a change in the basic appearance of a document is required. For example, single spacing may be changed to double spacing, margins may be made wider or narrower, type style can be changed, and right-hand justified copy can be changed to ragged right-hand copy. All of these changes require a complete rekeyboarding operation on a typewriter. Word processing systems make these changes automatically. The operator need only display the document on the display screen, set new margins, enter a justify or unjustify code, change the line spacing command, or change the type font on the system printer. Once this is done, typically taking less than a minute, the document can be played out in its new form. The advantages in reformatting provided by a word processing system over a typewriter are incomparable:

Reformatting is simple

1. Less keyboarding time—automatic features allow document reformatting to be achieved in a matter of seconds.
2. Higher-quality output—reformatted material can be inspected and adjusted on the display

screen to ensure accurate arrangement before final playout.

WP savings

3. Faster turnaround—material can be reformatted in a matter of seconds and played out on the system's high-speed printer; the benefits attributed to iterative documents also apply.

4-33. Financial Documents. Financial documents containing rows and columns of numbers are often time-consuming when prepared on a standard typewriter. Features offered by word processing systems make these documents much easier to prepare. Two features in particular are quite valuable: the decimal tab and the mathematical support package.

Automatic decimal alignment

The decimal tab feature automatically aligns decimal points vertically so that all numbers are positioned properly. The operator simply tabs from column to column and types in numbers and decimal points without worrying about alignment.

The system does the math

Mathematical support packages are used to perform computations on numbers entered on the display screen. Many add, subtract, multiply, and divide and can execute fairly complex equations. Many are designed to sum row and column values and enter answers in predesignated positions. One popular mathematical support feature is crossfooting, where rows and columns are added and totaled simultaneously. Some mathematical packages are easy to use, and most operators can employ them with minimum training. Others are quite complex and require specialized training in order for the operator to be able to write equations for computing numbers and displaying answers.

The decimal tab and mathematical support features make word processing systems extremely productive compared to standard typewriters in business operations where the preparation of financial data is done regularly. Advantages offered by word processing systems over standard typewriters include

1. Less keyboarding time—automatic centering and decimal tab features eliminate excessive alignment time; column headings can be moved from page to page through a system copy feature to eliminate retyping of identical text.

2. Higher-quality output—mathematical support features ensure accurate calculations and cross-footing; this ensures that answers will be right (if proper data are entered) and eliminates the need to verify answers.

WP savings

3. Faster turnaround—the mathematical support feature allows computations to be achieved in a fraction of the time required for hand calculations; the benefits attributed to iterative documents also apply when changes are required.

4-34. Ask the Right Questions

Each kind of business has varied problems that are solved in different ways. There is no single solution that can be applied to every problem. It takes people who know the business to determine what the best solutions are. That's one of the principal reasons for this book. As a business manager, you are the expert. By knowing what word processing systems can do, you can come up with ways to apply word processing features to your problems. An important benefit of this book is that it arms you with enough information about equipment and features to ask good questions. Armed with the right questions, you'll be able to zero in on specific areas of interest without wasting time floundering around looking at equipment and features that are of no concern. Don't let the salesman tell you what you need; you know what you need! It's you who must describe what's needed to the salesman. His job is to get the right answers to your

You're the expert

questions, demonstrate system features that apply to your problems, describe why his company is qualified to support your requirements, and quote price and delivery.

You'll be ready

Chapter 9 includes some information on how to get the most out of your word processing salesman. By the time you reach Chapter 9, you'll be ready to make a long list of the right questions that should save both you and your salesman a considerable amount of time.

5 The Nuts and Bolts of Text Processing

5-1. INTRODUCTION

This chapter describes word processing system text-editing features. Much of the information is condensed in tabular form for quick reference. The tables can be used to develop your own personal check list while looking at word processing systems and comparing features.

When analyzing word processing systems, many things must be considered. These include

1. Functional applicability
2. File storage and retrieval
3. Prompts and menus (learning aids)
4. Repertoire of features
5. Display size
6. Reliability
7. Impact on business costs and productivity

8. Price or lease level
9. User documentation (instruction manuals, reference cards, etc.)
10. Operator training
11. Service
12. Upgradability
13. Document security (limited access)

Some WP considerations

14. Physical flexibility (portability and adaptability)
15. Environmental impact (noise, size, heat)
16. Compatibility with other equipment and systems
17. Storage capacity (filing size)
18. Optional equipment offered
19. Availability of operating supplies
20. Functional speed.

These are not necessarily all the things to be considered, but the list makes a good start. All of these items are discussed in this book to some degree. In this chapter, file storage and retrieval, prompts and menus, repertoire of features, and display size are addressed.

5-2. FILE STORAGE AND RETRIEVAL

Determine the ease of storage and retrieval

When reviewing word processor system functionality, it is important to determine the ease of filing and retrieving documents. This is a transaction that is sometimes overlooked, and after all, every operator must go through filing and retrieving many times each day. Most modern word processing systems offer document indexes. These indexes act as a table of contents for all documents filed on the system's storage medium (disk or tape).

5-3. Media Storage Capacity

The storage capacity of systems vary, depending on the type and size of storage medium used. As mentioned earlier in the book, magnetic tape cassettes and magnetic disks are used extensively. Magnetic disks are the most popular storage devices because of their size, storage density, and ease of accessing information. Disk drive units can index to information rapidly by simply scanning the surface of the medium for the right data. Tape must be searched from end to end, making data access much slower. There has been a proliferation of disk configurations, and each configuration is a different size with a different storage capacity. A few common disk types:

Disks the most rapid

- Eight-inch, single-sided floppy disk
- Single-sided miniature disk
- Double-sided, single-density disk
- Double-sided, dual-density disk
- 2.5-megabyte hard disk (2,500,000 characters)
- 5-megabyte hard disk (5,000,000 characters)
- 10-megabyte hard disk (10,000,000 characters)

Some disk types

Figure 5-1. A Typical Eight-Inch Flexible Diskette

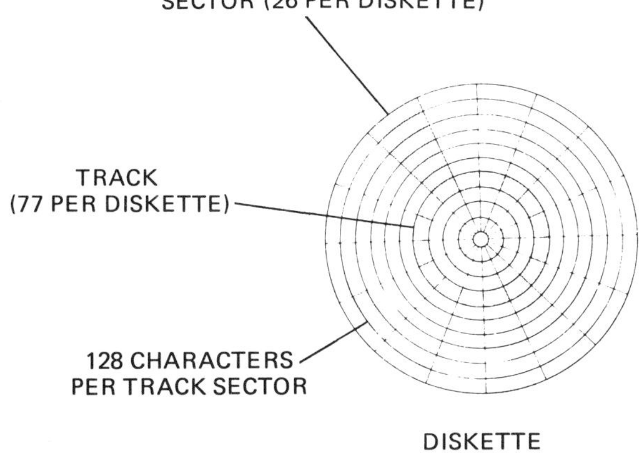

Figure 5-1 shows a typical eight-inch, single-sided flexible diskette. The figure illustrates how the disk is organized and how data is filed in tracks and sectors.

5-4. File Indexes

Storage varies with media

Word processing system files vary from small, partial-page documents to large, multipage documents. For example, a small document can be something like a name and address for a mailing label. A large document can be a lengthy report or a book. The type of storage medium used by a word processing system determines how many documents can be stored. For example, a floppy disk can store anywhere from the equivalent of 50 to 120 8½-by-11-inch pages of information. If a system has an eighty-page storage capacity and the average document size is two pages, the disk will be full at forty documents. Systems that use large storage devices, such as a ten-megabyte hard disk, can store up to four thousand pages.

Regardless of the storage medium size, there are several things that a word processing system operator needs to know about filed documents:

Document file information

1. Document identification number
2. Document title
3. Document size
4. Last document filing date.

Most word processing systems use file indexes that list the above information. Some systems automatically assign document numbers to text files while others allow the operator to assign a number. Document titles are assigned by operators either when the document is filed or prior to its creation. Many systems have space limitations on title lengths. If the space is limited to sixteen characters, for example, the operator simply uses abbreviated document titles.

Document size is displayed on some system file indexes, expressed either in pages or keystrokes. Knowing the size of a filed document can be helpful to an operator who is required to review a file index containing documents created by someone else.

Knowing when a document was last filed is often helpful in file maintenance. If a document has been dormant for more than ninety or 120 days, it may be eligible for deletion from the disk to make room for active documents. In addition, when several versions of a document exist, knowing which version was filed last lets the operator know which one is most current.

Some systems inefficient

Some word processing systems aren't equipped with automatic file indexes. On these systems operators must either create a document on the system that acts as a file index or record all document identification information on a sheet of paper. In either case, the lack of an index is often unwieldy, and retrieval can be difficult if the index document is lost.

5-5. PROMPTS AND MENUS

WP messages and recipes

Well-designed word processing systems interact with operators through messages, called *prompts*, and lists of information, called *menus*, that act as recipes to guide an operator through particular machine operations. The next two paragraphs describe the use of prompts and menus.

5-6. Prompts

Prompts are system messages that are displayed on the screen for the system operator to read. When displayed, prompts are frequently accompanied by a system tone to alert the operator to read the prompt message.

Two kinds of prompts

There are two general kinds of prompts used on word processing systems: informative prompts and action prompts. Informative prompts communicate with system operators to let them know when the system is performing some system function or to alert them to some illegal keystroke entry. For example, in response to the entry of an invalid keystroke sequence, the machine may simply display the message "INVALID KEY SEQUENCE."

Action prompts require operator response. These prompts are used to guide operators through a machine operation. For instance, when an operator moves a block of text, he or she may start by pressing the MOVE key. When this is done, a prompt saying "MOVE WHAT?" appears. When the operator selects the text to be moved, a prompt saying "TO WHERE?" appears. The process continues until the operator completes the transaction.

5-7. Menus

Good menus helpful

Well-designed menus are extremely helpful in guiding word processing system operators through complex functions. Menus, which are displayed on the word processing system's screen, are typically developed to assist operators when performing functions that require rather complex sequences of keystrokes or operator decisions. Typical functions using menus include

1. Printing
2. Document creation and filing
3. Telecommunicating
4. Sorting
5. Performing mathematical computations
6. Document and disk copying.

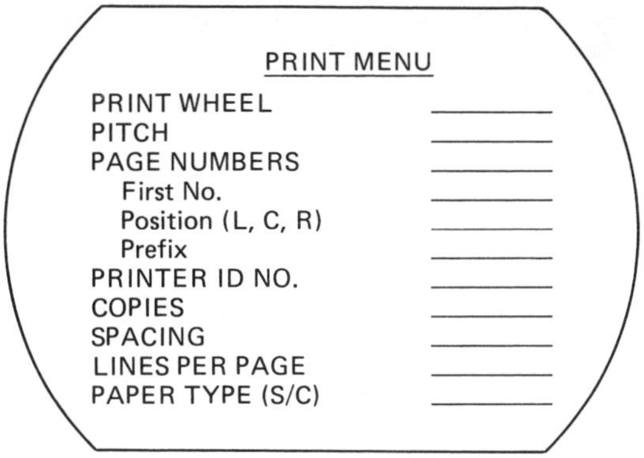

PRINT MENU

PRINT WHEEL	________
PITCH	________
PAGE NUMBERS	________
First No.	________
Position (L, C, R)	________
Prefix	________
PRINTER ID NO.	________
COPIES	________
SPACING	________
LINES PER PAGE	________
PAPER TYPE (S/C)	________

Figure 5-2. Information Contained on a Typical Print Menu

A typical print menu is shown in Figure 5-2.

When using a menu, an operator normally moves through it in order, inserting answers to menu questions (blanks) from the keyboard. Often, questions already have *system default* answers in place. These system defaults keep the operator from having to respond to every question in the menu. Default answers are intended to be the most common ones used. For instance, print menus often give the operator a choice of ten- or twelve-pitch type. If the word processing system usually uses twelve pitch, the default entry would be set to "12." This lets the operator change only those menu parameters that are different than normal. Often, operators can use all menu defaults directly. In the case of a print menu, they can simply execute the print command without having to spend extensive time interacting with the menu.

Defaults contain the most common menu responses

5-8. FORMAT CONTROL

All word processing systems have the ability to control margins, page length, and line spacing, which are all document format control features. Type size, tabs, right-hand justification, and automatic hyphenation are also format features offered by word processing systems.

WP formatting easy

```
Document  0116A  Now on Page  20  Line  34  Position  57
_|1....▶.....▶.....▶...▶....▶....▶.....▶.................................◀
```

Figure 5-3. Typical Format Status Line

5-9. Format Status Lines

Showing format on the screen

Format status lines are often displayed at the top or bottom of the display screen so that system operators can refer to and adjust document format as documents are created or edited. Systems that allow multiple formats to be used on documents often display two or more format status lines in the text area to show where format changes occur. An example of a format status line is shown in Figure 5-3. Note that in addition to document format information, the document number, page, and cursor position are also shown.

5-10. Text Visualization

Most systems provide a facsimile of the output format on the screen, letting the operator visualize what the document will look like before it is printed. This includes upper- and lowercase characters, line length, line spacing (or blank lines), indentations, tabular columns, and centered text.

Special format symbols helpful

5-11. Displaying Special Format Symbols. Some word processing systems display only text, numeric, and punctuation characters. Others display special symbols representing tabs, line returns, blank spaces, centering, and other keystrokes that are transparent when printed. These special format symbols, which are normally easy to learn, can be helpful when setting up a page of text. Operators can see exactly where and how many regular tabs, decimal tabs, indents, and blank spaces exist in a document. Examples of some of the special characters are shown in this list.

Symbol	Meaning
•	Blank Space
◆	Center
•̲	Decimal Tab
→	Indent
◄	Line Return
↕	Merge
⊥	Page ending
►	Standard Tab
↑	Superscript
↓	Subscript

5-12. Full-Page and Partial-Page Displays. The purpose of full-page displays is to provide a one-to-one relationship between a printed page and the page image shown on the system's display screen. The full-page display lets operators see an entire page at a time. Partial-page displays normally have anywhere from a dozen to twenty-four lines per *screenload*. If the partial-page system displays twenty lines per screenload, three screenloads will have to be viewed to see the contents of an entire page. Well-designed partial-page systems normally carry over a few lines of text from previous screens to allow operators to keep track of where they are in the text or on the page. In discussing the relative convenience of partial-page and full-page displays with word processing system operators, most who have used both seem to have no strong preference.

A full-page display may be desirable

Table 5-1. Word Processing System Format Terms and Definitions

Term	Definition
Decimal or Align Tab	Similar to the standard tab except that decimals rather than left-hand margins are aligned in columns. Used extensively in financial tables where dollar-and-cents notation is used. Also can be used to align right-hand margin of columns where no decimal or period is used.
Line spacing	Space between lines of text. Standard single spacing is six lines per inch. Double spacing is three lines per inch. Spacing possibilities include single, one and one half, double, and triple.

Table 5-1 (continued)

Term	Definition
Margin	Right- and left-hand margin location. Controls line length and white space from edge of paper to text.
Page length	Length of text from top to bottom of a page. On standard 8½-by-11-inch paper, fifty-four lines of text make a page nine inches long, leaving one inch of white space at top and bottom.
Ragged right-hand margin	Unjustified right-hand margin. Printed page has standard typewriter appearance.
Reformat	To change standard format settings such as margins (page width), lines per page (page length), tab locations, etc.
Right-hand justification	System feature that automatically aligns right-hand margin of text. Varies from system to system in that some systems insert blank spaces between words to achieve uniform line length while others insert units of space between characters in words. The former method sometimes leaves vertical "valleys" of white space on a page. The latter method eliminates valleys.
Tab (standard)	Operator-selectable location point (or points) on a line of text. Tabs let the operator advance to preset positions by pressing a tab key. Used heavily in tables and other documents with multiple columns where the left-hand margin of columns are aligned on the tab position.
Type size	The standard for letter-quality printers is the number of text characters per inch measured in pitch. Common measures are eight, ten, and twelve pitch, which means eight, ten, and twelve characters per inch. (Some systems allow any pitch size desired for special effects.) Proportional spacing type size is also selectable on some systems. Instead of a fixed number of characters per inch, the characters occupy space according to their size. An "i" may occupy two units of space while a "W" may occupy five units. Proportional type usually has a more pleasing appearance than *monospace* (pitch-measured) type. Typesetters use a completely different type size system, where type is measured in points (seventy-two points per inch) and varies in both size and spacing.
Type style	The shape and boldness of typed characters, such as gothic, block, italic, or any of hundreds of other type configurations.

Table 5-2. Common Word Processing System Editing Terms and Definitions

Term	Definitions
Blank (destructive space)	A key, which on some systems is the space bar, that enters a blank space at the cursor position.
Copy or duplicate	Feature which provides the ability to copy (duplicate) text from one location in a document to another. Some systems allow text to be copied from one document to another. When material is copied the original text is left intact. When the copied material is inserted at the selected location, the system normally readjusts text to accommodate the added text automatically.
Cursor control	Feature which provides the ability to position a character marker (cursor) on the display screen from special keys on the keyboard. The cursor, which is either a bright underscore line or a character-sized rectangle of light, marks the position for character entry from the keyboard. There are normally seven keys that control the cursor: the space bar, return key, backspace key, and north (up arrow), south (down arrow), east (right arrow), and west (left arrow) keys.
Delete	Feature which provides the ability to delete (eliminate) a space, character, series of characters and spaces, line, paragraph, or page. When material is deleted from a document, the system normally readjusts (closes up) remaining text automatically.
Insert	Feature which provides the ability to insert (add) a space, character, series of characters and spaces, line, paragraph, or page. When material is inserted in a document, the system normally readjusts text to accommodate the added text automatically.
Move	Feature which provides the ability to move (relocate) text from one location in a document to another. Some systems allow text to be moved from one document to another. When material is moved, the system normally readjusts affected text by closing up the area from which the text was taken and adjusting the text at the new position to accommodate the added text.
Strikeover	Feature which will position the cursor over any text or punctuation character or blank space on the display screen and permit its replacement with another.

5-13. Format Definitions

Table 5-1 contains a list of format terms and definitions for quick reference.

5-14. COMMON EDITING FUNCTIONS

System activity should be transparent

This section addresses common editing functions that exist on most word processing systems. Good word processing systems make keyboard work as straightforward as possible. Machine operation should seem as close as possible to typing material on a standard typewriter. System activity should be transparent to operators, whose primary concern is simply creating or editing text. If they have to go through complex sequences of keystrokes, count text line numbers, and perform other special, time-consuming tasks to insert, move, or delete text, then the word processing system is probably not very well designed. Table 5-2 contains a list of common editing function terms and definitions.

5-15. OTHER WORD PROCESSING FEATURES

Know what's standard

Claims may not be there

This section describes word processing system features that are standard on some systems and offered as options on others. It's important to know what is standard (you get these at no additional charge) and what is optional. Of course it will be extremely important for you to know which ones will have significant impact on the productivity of your operation. Be sure that you've looked at the important features closely. You may find that manufacturers' claims are not what they seem on the surface. What might be a relatively simple feature on one system might be complex and time-consuming on another. A good example of this is mathematical support packages. On some systems it is very easy to add rows and columns of numbers and insert answers in the text. Other mathematical support packages require extensive programing activity which is sufficiently rigorous to discourage system operators from ever using them. Table 5-3 contains a list of terms and definitions of these features.

Table 5-3. Other Word Processing System Feature Terms and Definitions

Term	Definition
Automatic features:	
Carrier return	Used with free-form typing. Automatically wraps words that exceed the right-hand margin limit to the next line. Eliminates the necessity for the operator to use the return key.
Centering	Allows centering of text between the margins or over a fixed point or points on a line. Should be achieved by pressing either a CENTER key or a special two-key sequence.
Double underscore	Automatically inserts a double underscore at specified locations during printout.
Footnotes	Allows the operator to enter footnote information in the body of the text and then automatically moves it to the bottom of the page in its proper form.
Headers and footers	Prints *running heads and feet* (standard text used at the top and bottom of each page in a document) at proper locations during printout.
Hyphenation	Alerts the operator at the end of each line where a hyphen may be required. Once the operator makes a decision, the line is automatically right-hand justified to the hyphen. Also gives the operator the option of eliminating the hyphen entirely by rejustifying the line and transferring the entire word to the following line.
Multistrike or bold print	Automatically double- or triple-strikes specified text during printout to ensure bold characters. Used heavily on viewgraphs (overhead projection documents) where dark, bold lettering is desirable.
Page numbering	During the printing operation, automatically inserts sequential page numbers at the bottom of the page. Some systems allow number prefixes and number location (bottom left, center, or right) plus line location or distance below text.
Underscore and deunderscore	Underscore underlines automatically as the text is typed or automatically underscores specified sections of the text. Deunderscore eliminates the underscore function during typing. On some systems, eliminates the underscore from specified sections of the text.

Table 5-3 (continued)

Term	Definition
Column editing	Allows columns of text in tables to be inserted, deleted, moved, or exchanged. This is an important feature in operations that use tabular material extensively.
Document assembly	Allows specified portions of text from various documents to be assembled into a new document. For example, a law firm may assemble filed contract clauses and excerpts from a list of terms and conditions in generating a new contract.
Form entry	Provides operators with a guide for filling out preprinted forms by allowing a form to be displayed and a mask created. One approach allows a preprinted form to be placed on the printer and filled out from the keyboard as on a standard typewriter. In this way line spacing and text lengths are correlated between the printer and the display screen. This is not a common feature.
Form letter	Allows a form letter with blank spaces for variable information to be created and displayed. The form letter, referred to as a *mask* or *base document*, is displayed and filled in for each set of variable text (name, address, date, etc.).
Global pagination or repagination	Automatically adjusts all pages within a document to a specified page length (usually a certain number of lines). Some systems automatically assign page numbers through global pagination.
Global replace	Automatically replaces a specified character string throughout an entire document. For example, a part number or name might be changed throughout the text using global replace.
Global search	Automatically locates and highlights a specified character string throughout an entire document. Can be used to determine how many times a certain word or phrase is used in a document.
Global search and replace	Automatically locates and highlights a specified character string throughout an entire document. May give the operator the option of replacing or leaving the specified character string prior to moving to the next occurrence. This is almost identical to global replace except for the operator option.

Table 5-3 (continued)

Term	Definition
Glossary or user defined keys	A special document prepared and filed on some word processing systems created to eliminate often-used keystrokes. For example, if a number of long terms or phrases are used frequently in text, they can be recalled and inserted into the document with only two or three keystrokes.
Graphics	Allows limited line drawing. Normally restricted to a standard typewriter character set which uses the underscore for drawing horizontal lines and the exclamation mark (!) for drawing vertical lines. Some systems do offer a vertical rule character. Frequently used in creating organization charts and block diagrams.
Mathematical support package	Makes mathematical computations such as adding rows and columns of numbers and inserting the answers in operator-designated locations. Usually used in conjunction with align or decimal tabs. Some systems add, subtract, multiply, divide, and insert parentheses or minus signs for negative values. This feature is often referred to as *Mathpak*.
Merge	Combines a list of variables into a base document. This function, sometimes called *list-merge*, will automatically print the base document and variables as many times as necessary until all sets of variables are used. It precludes the need to display and fill in a form letter for each set of variables.
Replace	Allows a character or string of characters (called *character string*) to be replaced with another character or character string. The replace feature allows a character string of a different length than the original to be used. Text adjustment is automatically made to accommodate the new text.
Scrolling	Moves text horizontally (*horizontal scroll*) or vertically (*vertical scroll*), as required, to see information that is beyond the physical character capacity of the display screen. For example, if a system display screen is limited to eighty characters by twenty-one lines, the scrolling feature can let the operator scroll the text up and to the left to look at text located on line 48, character position 105 of a text page.

Table 5-3 (continued)

Term	Definition
Search	Automatically locates a specified character string within a document. Normally used by pressing a special key or key sequence, typing in the character string being sought, and allowing the system to advance rapidly through a document until the character string is located and highlighted. *Highlighting* is when a portion of text is made brighter than the rest of the text for easy identification.
Sort	Arranges specified characters in alphabetical, numerical, or alphanumerical order. Can be either ascending (A to Z) or descending (Z to A) order.
Stop code	Provides for printer control during printout of a document using multiple type styles. For example, if a page of text has an italicized passage, a stop code is imbedded in the text to stop the printer for a type change. Once the italic passage is complete, another stop code is used to stop the printer, allowing the operator to change back to the original type style. Stop codes normally appear on the screen as a special character.
Strike through or overprint	Allows an operator to type a sequence that instructs the printer to type two characters in one space. Frequently used to show deleted text in a document.
Superscripts and subscripts	Indexes text characters up or down as needed to effect superscripts and subscripts during printing. Usually accomplished through the use of special key or key sequence. For example, "H_2O" uses a subscript 2.
System security	Prevents unauthorized access to documents containing personal or private information. Documents are *password-protected;* that is, they require the entry of an operator-developed password (key sequence) before they can be retrieved from storage for display, editing, or printing purposes.
Telecommunications	Allows a word processing system to communicate with other word processing systems, data processing systems, or photocomposition systems via telephone lines.
Top of form or reverse roll	Allows an operator to type a sequence that instructs the printer to reverse line feed to the top of the page. Used for two-column or multiple type style text preparation.

Table 5-3 (continued)

Term	Definition
Type-through or direct keyboard mode	Allows an operator to type from the work station keyboard while the printer simultaneously outputs the keystrokes on paper. This allows an operator to use the word processing system like a standard typewriter. This feature can be particularly handy for typing small labels or preprinted forms. This is not a common feature.

6

Text Processing Input and Output

6-1. INTRODUCTION

This chapter describes common word processing system input and output devices that the business manager should be familiar with when considering which tools are best suited for the tasks at hand. Included with the descriptions of input devices are some thoughts about human factors and the generation of special symbols. The description of output devices includes information about common output devices, photocomposers, type measurement and quality, and output media.

Common devices described

6-2. COMMON INPUT DEVICES

There are a variety of word processing system input devices. Chapter 3 described various types of word processing systems which included a brief description of some of the most common types of input terminals. Some of these are

1. Keyboard terminals
2. Keyboard–cathode ray tube (CRT) display terminals

Some WP input devices

3. Keyboard–strip display terminals
4. Keyboard–mini-CRT display terminals
5. Media input terminals
6. Optical character readers.

6-3. Keyboard Terminals

Corrections made on media

These terminals are very similar to a typewriter. As the keystrokes are typed out on paper in the terminal's printer mechanism, they are simultaneously recorded on a magnetic medium in tape, card, or disk form. Inserts, deletes, and strikeovers can be made from the keyboard on the magnetic medium to reflect editorial changes. Once the affected areas are corrected, a letter-perfect copy can be played out.

6-4. Keyboard–Cathode Ray Tube (CRT) Display Terminals

This is the common terminal for display-based word processing systems. A description of the difference between full-page and partial-page displays is contained in paragraph 5-12. A picture of a typical par-

Figure 6-1. A Partial-Page CRT Display Work Station

Figure 6-2. A Full-Page CRT Display Work Station

tial-page keyboard-CRT terminal is shown in Figure 6-1. A full-page display is shown in Figure 6-2. These terminals display the keyboarded characters on a display screen allowing the operator to strike over, insert, delete, move, copy, and perform other text-editing functions before a document is ever printed on paper.

Displaying text saves paper

Figure 6-3 shows a diagram of how a keyboard-CRT terminal typically interacts in a word processing system. The screen acts as a storage device. As the screen fills up, text overflows to the system's memory. Once the text is complete, it is filed from memory to the system's storage medium, which is usually a mag-

Test flow between screen, memory, and medium

Figure 6-3. Typical Word Processing System Data Flow

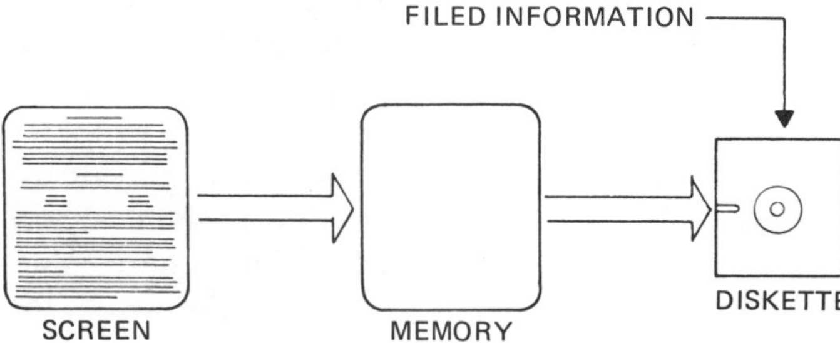

netic tape or disk. When a document is recalled from the system's magnetic medium, it is loaded into memory. It is then retrieved from memory to the display screen for editing.

6-5. Keyboard–Strip Display Terminals

These terminals are more compact than the keyboard-CRT terminals since they do not have a large display package. Like the other terminals, these also use magnetic media to record keystrokes. The display precludes the need to use paper to catch inputted copy. Since the display is usually quite small (strip systems typically display around fifty characters), vertical alignment of text must usually be verified on paper.

Strip display units more compact

6-6. Limited-Line CRT Display Terminals

There are a few systems in production that use small CRT displays that are limited to a small number of lines of text. These systems are functionally somewhere between a full-blown keyboard–CRT display terminal and keyboard–strip display terminal. The small size of the CRT and its associated electronics package normally makes these systems compact, lightweight, and relatively inexpensive. Many business managers believe that they are well suited to a host of office applications.

Small CRT displays

6-7. Media Input Terminals

There are some terminals that are used to capture keystrokes on media that have no electrical connection to a central word processing system CPU. When these systems are used, the documents are prepared on a magnetic medium, the medium is physically transferred to the word processing system, which outputs the document on paper. When changes are required, the medium is returned to the input terminal, where editing takes place. Once the text is changed, the medium is once again physically transferred to the word processing system, where the revised document is printed out. This approach to *off-line* medium preparation is very common on photocomposition systems. The cost of media-preparation devices is normally one third to one half that of a full-blown word processing system with output capability.

Off-line document preparation

6-8. Optical Character Readers (OCRs)

These devices have been in use for several years, and in some installations they have a great deal of merit. Basically, OCRs scan typed characters optically, convert the scanned document to machine-recognizable data codes, and store the document on the system's storage medium. This allows the document to be called up on a standard word processing terminal for text editing or to be printed on the system's output device. OCRs can be used to

Putting printed matter in the system

1. Consolidate text inputs from various systems into a single system
2. Allow existing standard typewriters to act as keyboard work stations for the OCR-connected word processing system
3. Input preprinted or pretyped documents into the OCR-connected word processing system
4. Reformat preprinted or pretyped documents by inputting through the OCR and outputting on the system's printer.

When considering an OCR, it is important to understand exactly what style of characters the equipment can read. Some are limited to a specific type style and size. This means that all existing typewriters and printers must be equipped with the prescribed type style to be compatible with the OCR. Some OCRs can

Know what the OCR reads

be programed to read conventional type styles. These systems are more flexible, but they require conversion time prior to reading different type styles. Regardless of the type of OCR selected, ensure that compatibility is fully understood and tested before making your final choice.

6-9. Human Factors and Input Methods

The development of every good word processing system input device should include considerable attention to human factors. Well-designed equipment is easy to use; easy-to-use equipment is more productive. Most manufacturers spend a great deal of time determining

Human considerations vital

1. Keyboard layout
2. Character set
3. Screen size and angle
4. Readability
5. Color.

6-10. Determining Input-Terminal Comfort. One of the best tests for an input terminal is to have a few experienced operators sit down and try it out. If the keyboard touch is comfortable, access to special keys easy, and visibility pleasing, they'll be the first to know. If it's not, they'll be the first to tell you about it. To make it a fair test, be sure that the terminal is on a desk or table of the right height, check to see that the operator's chair is properly adjusted, and verify that the surrounding environment is quiet, cool, and clean. If the area is comfortable, the operators will be able to concentrate on the keyboard. If it is not, they may unconsciously associate their general discomfort with the system they are trying.

Make sure they're comfortable

6-11. Keyboard Control Systems. Another factor in the ease of use of a word processing system keyboard is the design of key sequences used to control system functions. There are three basic types of keyboard control systems:

1. Mnemonic systems
2. Code key systems
3. Combination mnemonic and code key systems.

Keystroke methods

The mnemonic keyboard system uses a sequence of keystrokes which includes the use of character keys to execute a system function. Mnemonic instructions normally start with a special function key, which alerts the system that the following character or sequence of characters is a special instruction. For example, to insert a stop code, a system might require pressing the SPECIAL FUNCTION key (sometimes called CONTROL key), the S key, and the EXECUTE key. To execute a centering command, the SPECIAL FUNCTION and C keys may be the ones used. Word processing systems that use mnemonics have a limited set of special keys. The character keys used normally have some relationship to the function being performed. The C key may be used for centering, the underscore key for autoscore, the = key for mathematics, and the S key for stop code. Even though mnemonic keyboard systems are designed to eliminate special code keys, they usually have CANCEL, EXECUTE, NORTH (up arrow), SOUTH (down arrow), EAST (right arrow), and WEST (left arrow) keys. Mnemonic systems are sometimes a little more difficult to learn than other systems since operators must memorize a number of special key sequences. However, they can be made easier by choosing mnemonics that are straightforward.

Straightforward mnemonics important

Code key systems use special keys, located on the keyboard beside and above the standard character set, to execute word processing system functions.

Keyboards on these systems may have twenty or more labeled code keys. Some common code keys used include

Typical code keys

INSERT
DELETE
MOVE
COPY
INDENT
PAGE
CENTER
DECIMAL TAB
MERGE
STOP
SEARCH
REPLACE
GO TO PAGE . . .

Code key systems are normally quite easy to learn, since the special system functions can be read directly from the key caps. A picture of a code key system keyboard is shown in Figure 6-4.

Combination mnemonic–code key systems are most commonly used. These systems use a mixture of spe-

Figure 6-4. A Code Key Word Processing System Keyboard

Figure 6-5. A Combination Mnemonic–Code Key Keyboard

cial code keys and character keys to perform system functions. For example, the system may use all special code keys to perform frequently used functions such as insert, delete, move, and print. A combination of SPECIAL FUNCTION and character keys may be used for less frequently used functions. To set a decimal tab on a combination mnemonic–code key system, the SPECIAL FUNCTION and D keys may be used. A typical combination mnemonic–code key system keyboard is shown in Figure 6-5.

A combination most common

6-12. Using Special Symbols

Some business operations require the use of special mathematical, Greek, and graphic symbols. There are several approaches to obtaining special symbols, including

1. Direct keyboard entry
2. Look-up tables
3. Graphic aids.

Approaches to special symbols

The following three paragraphs describe these three methods.

The easiest way

6-13. Direct Keyboard Entry of Special Symbols. Some word processing systems support special characters on the input terminal's display screen and have matching type on their output devices. When this is the case, the use of special symbols is easy, since they can be entered directly from the keyboard. These systems normally have specially engraved key caps to show which keys to use for the various special symbols. To access the special symbols, a special function key is used to designate alternate key functions. Often, special symbol fonts must be used to match the special character symbols. This requires imbedding printer stop codes in the text at the point of special symbol use. When the printer reaches the stop code, the special symbol font can be inserted and the printer restarted. Another stop code is used when it is time to change the type font back to the original text style.

Changing print wheels often necessary

Some systems use a *top-of-form* (or reverse-roll) approach to multifont printing. This allows all text of one style to be typed on a page, leaving blank space where special symbols are to be inserted. Once the standard character set is printed, the printer reverses direction and rolls to the top of the sheet of paper. At this point the operator inserts the special symbol font, and the printer restarts, printing all the special symbols. This method eliminates the need for the operator to change the type font each time a special symbol is used on a page.

Minimizing font changes

6-14. Look-Up Tables for Special Symbols. Most word processing systems have standard character set keyboards and only display standard alphabetical, numerical, and punctuation characters on their display screens. However, many of these word processing systems can still output special symbols through the use of special symbol type fonts. The relative position between special symbols on the type font and standard characters on the keyboard must be known by the operator during the keyboarding operation. A map of the keyboard and the corresponding special

Relative position charts

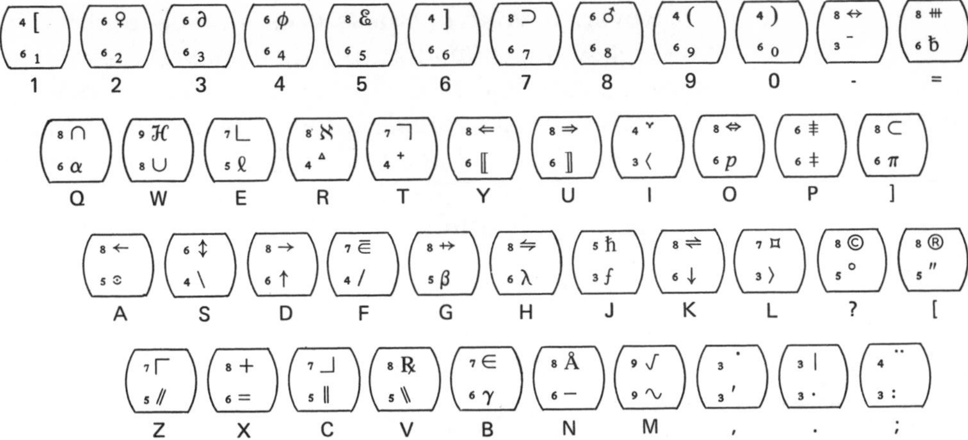

Figure 6-6. A Typical Keyboard Look-Up Table

symbols, called a *look-up table*, is used as a reference tool by the operator when typing special symbol documents. Figure 6-6 shows a typical look-up table.

6-15. Graphic Aids for Special Symbols. When special symbols are used infrequently, there are a number of manufacturers that offer special symbol transfer sheets. These sheets contain various Greek and mathematical symbols that can be transferred by simply laying the transparent transfer sheet over the document being prepared, rubbing the back of the sheet with a burnishing tool or a soft pencil, and pulling the sheet up and away from the document. The symbol sticks to the document by means of a tacky wax substance. When preparing documents for use with transfer sheets, the operator simply leaves blank space where the symbol transfer is to be made. There are some transfer sheet vendors that will make custom transfer sheets to your specifications. This includes sheets that feature special trademarks and logos. If your company has a large graphics lab, there are commercially available materials that allow you to fabricate transfer sheets of your own.

An old method still in use

Making your own graphics is possible

The use of transfer sheets is probably the most time-consuming method of incorporating special symbols.

However, if your business uses a small number of special symbols on an infrequent basis, it may be the most economical in the long run, since systems that support special symbols directly are often quite expensive. Your cost analysis will give you the answer to what is economically feasible for your particular business application.

Analyze the trade-off

6-16. COMMON OUTPUT DEVICES

There are several word processing system output devices. These include

Some WP output devices

1. Impact printers
2. Thermal printers
3. Ink jet printers
4. Laser printers
5. Intelligent copiers
6. Photocomposers.

All of these output devices employ different technologies. In this section, a brief description of the functionality and application of each family of output devices is provided.

6-17. Impact Printers

The most common printer

Impact printers have been around for a number of years. These printers strike a ribbon with character impressions, transferring that impression to paper. The original key-bar typewriter was an impact printer. IBM's Selectric typewriter, which uses a spherical type font, is an impact printer also. Other impact printer types include daisy wheel printers, thimble printers, matrix printers, and line printers.

6-18. Printer Speed. Selectric printers operate in the neighborhood of 175 words per minute, daisy wheel and thimble printers at about forty characters per second, and many high-speed line printers in excess of one thousand lines of text per minute. All these are interesting numbers, but printer speed is rarely a critical factor. Even the slowest printer is considerably faster than input speeds and will normally support between two and three input work stations comfortably. Of course, it's possible to overload a printer with too many input work stations or in an environment where many stored documents are printed repeatedly. When this is the case, faster printers or more printers may be the solution.

Output much faster than input

The line printer, which is the fastest printer listed, has been in use in data processing applications for many years. It is called a line printer because it prints an entire line of text at a time. Although line printers are extremely fast, the type quality is often poor in terms of style and density. However, in big operations where large numbers of internal review copies are required, a line printer can be a good choice. This leaves the letter-quality impact printers or photocomposers free for final output.

Sacrificing quality for speed

6-19. Printer Reliability. Reliability of a system is a function of the number of parts in it. This is true for both electronic and mechanical systems. It is particularly true for impact printers, which literally beat themselves to death. The old electric typewriters required constant service to keep them in top working order. Today's modern impact printers have fewer moving parts and therefore require less service; nevertheless, the word processor's impact printer is the single most trouble-prone component in the system and requires the most service calls.

They beat themselves to death

The daisy and thimble printers eliminated many of the moving parts used on older impact printers. The daisy printer, for example, has a type font, shown in Figure 6-7, that simply rotates. An electrical solenoid strikes the selected character petal (spoke), pressing it against the ribbon and transferring the character symbol to the paper. The thimble printer, which is similar in concept, is a rotating cylinder instead of

Reducing moving parts

Figure 6-7. Daisy Print Wheel

a wheel. The thimble printer has two rows of type instead of the usual single row of the daisy wheel. The second level of characters enables the thimble printer to support more characters than most standard daisy wheels. However, some daisy printers have multiple character rows allowing 128 characters on one wheel.

6-20. Matrix Printers

Speed may not be everything

Matrix printers use electrically driven pins that punch character representations through the unit's ribbon onto paper. For example, the letter "I" is made by a vertical column of pins. The "+" sign is made by a crossing vertical column and horizontal row of pins. These printers are faster than daisy and thimble printers and are quite reliable. However, the print quality is poor and they are quite noisy for an office environment. Their application is primarily in data processing, although some word processing manufacturers offer them.

6-21. Thermal Printers

Thermal printing technology has been around for many decades. The first devices to use thermal imaging were drum recorders and facsimile equipment. Many facsimile systems still use the thermal imaging principle today. Thermal printing is achieved by burning or scorching an image on sensitized paper. Facsimile uses a rotating drum and a line-scan principle. The voltage fed to the paper varies with the darkness of the image being scanned. The greater the voltage, the darker the line. Photographs can be copied, since tone gradations are transferred.

An old principle with a new twist

Thermal printers use a thermal matrix print head similar to the matrix printer in principle. The elements of the print head are heated to correspond to the selected character. Like the matrix printer, the letter "I" uses a vertical row of thermal elements. When these elements heat up, the treated paper is scorched. Thermal printers operate in the neighborhood of thirty characters per second. The print quality is relatively poor in terms of style and density. However, thermal printers are extremely quiet, making them ideally suited to some environments.

They're quiet

6-22. Ink Jet Printers

Ink jet printers have been in development since the early 1960s. However, they didn't reach a commercially acceptable status until the mid-1970s. Ink jet printing is used commercially in the carpet industry for dye application. It is also being used on drum printers for outputting computer graphics. The technology basically sprays ink, which has been configured electromagnetically into character shapes, onto the carrier medium. In the case of word processors, the medium is usually bond paper.

An emerging technology

Ink jet printing was introduced to the word processing industry by IBM. A high-speed ink jet printer was first offered on IBM's System 6. This printer is capable of printing a line a second and has special envelope-handling features. The system is a mechanical marvel to behold. It is used successfully in operations where form-letter work is the primary activity.

A close look

Upon close examination of characters printed by ink jet, you'll note that the quality of ink jet printing is not as good as letter-quality impact printing. Ragged edges can be seen on the character lines; this is particularly noticeable on diagonal lines. However, for most correspondence, the ink jet is quite acceptable.

6-23. Laser Printers

Another technology with potential

Like many technologies being adopted by the word processing industry, laser printing was developed for the data processing industry. This is an extremely high-speed printing method that burns character images onto a rotating drum by means of a laser beam. The heated surface area picks up toner, which is offset to paper. The characters are of extremely high quality. In fact, laser printing is sufficiently good to be used as a photocomposer output technology. The characters are dense, have smooth, clean edges, and a number of character styles and sizes can be selected. At this writing, laser printing is one of the most expensive output means. However, like other technologies, the price should decline as greater manufacturing volumes and corresponding experience are achieved.

6-24. Intelligent Copiers

An office time-saver with a big price tag

Intelligent copiers are offered by some word processing system manufacturers as a way to copy documents stored on the word processing system's storage media. These systems are fast, taking only a few seconds per page. They can prevent operators from having to carry paper masters of a document to a standard office copier, stand in line, hand-feed the document, and then bring the copies back for sorting.

Intelligent copiers can be hard-wired or telecommunication-connected to a word processing system. The word processing system simply transmits the document to the copier in the form of data. The copier's intelligence translates the received data into character images which are transferred to paper by a xerography process. Some copiers offer multiple character sets and are equipped with sorters which automatically collate multiple copies into sets. If your business is required to make large quantities of copies of material that is originated from keyboards, an intelligent copier may be a boost to productivity.

Good where lots of copies are needed

6-25. Photocomposers

Photocomposition, or phototypesetting, is used to set publication-quality type. These units, which have virtually replaced "hot lead" type, have been commercially available since the late 1960s. Photocomposers use light-sensitive paper similar to photographic print paper. This paper, once exposed by the photocomposer, must go through a development process. Type fonts are disk- or drum-shaped glass, plastic, or film, with clear type characters arranged concentrically around the font. A beam of light passes through the selected character, is channeled through an enlarging lens and fiber optics, and shines on the light-sensitive paper. The exposed area becomes a black character as the paper passes through the developing process.

Light beams and photographic paper do the trick

Photocomposers typically have four to eight different type styles on each changeable type font. The lens systems used enable these units to print a wide variety of type sizes by magnifying character images. Many can set type ranging from 5½ points (approximately 5/64 inch) up to 72 points (approximately one inch). If a type style is required that is different from the mounted type font, an operator can change it in less than a minute.

Type quality and versatility

Different types of paper are used in photocomposers. A variety of widths are offered, but eight-inch widths are the most popular for publication-format output. Newspapers use four-inch–width material since they work with narrow columns of text. In addition to coming in a variety of widths, paper comes in different chemical compositions as well. Relatively inexpensive stabilization-base paper turns yellow with age. If constantly exposed to room-level lighting, stabilization paper can lose its character images entirely in a matter of weeks or months, depending on the light intensity. This paper is ideal for use in newspapers and other operations where no requirement exists to store photocomposed masters beyond the printing time. If you wish to save photocomposed masters, slightly more expensive archival-quality, resin-coated paper can be used. The processor type and chemistry used to develop stabilization-base paper and resin-coated paper are different. It's important to determine which type of paper is best suited to your operation before purchasing or leasing the processing equipment and buying the supplies.

Choose the right paper and processor

6-26. Paper-Handling Equipment for Printers

Some manufacturers are offering paper-handling equipment to help save word processing system operator time. Two basic types of handlers exist:

Paper handlers

1. Continuous-form tractors
2. Automatic sheet feeders.

6-27. Continuous-Form Tractors. The continuous-form tractor, shown in Figure 6-8, is a device that can be attached to a letter-quality printer by the word processing system operator. It feeds continuous-form paper, which has pin holes on each edge, by means of a pin-feed mechanism. When mounted, the paper is automatically advanced as the document is printed. This is particularly convenient for multiple-page documents. The operator simply checks to see that the first page is properly aligned and executes the print command. The paper automatically ad-

Tractors save time

Figure 6-8. Continuous-Form Tractor

vances through the machine until the last page is printed. When complete, the operator removes the completed document. Continuous-form paper comes in many sizes and colors. Forms suppliers will make custom, preprinted continuous forms designed to suit specific needs. Of course, the expense of having special paper prepared should be warranted by volume and cost savings. The most popular paper is 8½-by-11-inch letter size.

This paper has horizontal perforations on eleven-inch centers and can be separated into standard page–size sheets. The edges are also perforated so that the pin-feed holes can be separated from the paper, leaving a standard 8½-inch-wide sheet.

6-28. Automatic Sheet Feeders. Automatic sheet feeders are devices that also mount on letter-quality printers. These units feed 8½-by-11-inch or legal-size bond paper into the printer. Rubber rollers are used to advance each sheet of paper beneath the printer platen and lower pressure rollers. Automatic sheet feeders are more expensive than form tractors, but they do save the time required to separate continuous-form sheets and can be used with standard letterhead stock.

Sheet feeders more expensive than tractors

6-29. Type Measurement

Two basic systems are used in measuring type. Letter-quality printers use pitch, typesetters use points. This paragraph briefly describes both systems.

6-30. Pitch Measure. Pitch measure was mentioned in Chapter 5. You may recall that pitch is the number of characters per inch on a horizontal line of text. Ten pitch, then, is ten characters per inch; twelve pitch is twelve characters per inch. Some systems are limited to ten and twelve pitch, while others can print almost any pitch entered from the keyboard. If a long name must be condensed to fit a small label, an operator may select fifteen pitch. The old typewriter terms *pica* and *elite* approximate ten and twelve pitch, respectively. Pitch measure is sometimes called monospace measure, since each character occupies one measure of space (1/10 or 1/12 inch).

10 pitch is "pica," 12 pitch is "elite"

There are a number of monospace type styles offered. Almost every word processing system manufacturer can give you a catalog of type styles offered on their system. Most manufacturers offer type styles that allow you to merge type from a word processing system printer with type from standard office typewriters.

6-31. Proportional Space Type. Proportional-space type, also mentioned in Chapter 5, has been around for many years. Typesetting uses proportional-space type. The IBM Executive typewriters that have been in use in offices for over twenty years also use proportional-space type. This measurement system lets each character occupy a certain amount of space in proportion to its size. On a proportional-space Executive typewriter, for example, an "i" uses two units of space, while a "W" uses five units. Proportional type is much more pleasing to the eye than monospace type, since the amount of white space between characters is more uniform.

Proportional-space type is prettier

6-32. Line Measure. The standard line measure on letter-quality printers is six lines per inch. An eleven-inch page, therefore, is sixty-six lines. If an operator wishes to have an inch of space at the top and bottom of a page, the selected line depth is fifty-four lines. Some printers offer extremely accurate control. They can index paper both horizontally and vertically in 1/100-inch increments. If this kind of accuracy is required, you should check around until you find a suitable vendor.

Impressive printer control available

6-33. Typesetting Measure. Type used on typesetters is proportional-space type, where each character occupies a certain amount of space in proportion to its size. The measure used, called points and pica, got its beginning with hot type, where lead was molded into fonts to form characters. Modern photocomposers still use this measure today, and photocomposition equipment operators must learn the system. A point is within a thousandth of an inch of being 1/72 inch. There are six picas to the inch. It follows, then, that there are twelve points per pica. A ten-point letter is approximately 10/72 inch high from the bottom of a descender to the top of an ascender. Figure 6-9 shows this relationship. Line length is expressed in picas. A forty-two-pica line is approximately seven inches long (42 ÷ 6 = 7).

The hot-type system still in use

The space between base lines is measured in points of *leading*, which is a carryover from the hot-type days. The instruction "set 10 on 12" means that a

Figure 6-9. Typesetting Measure

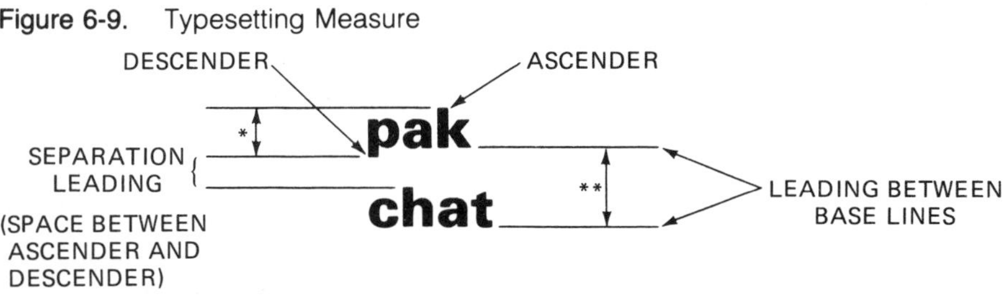

document is to have ten-point character size and twelve-point line spacing. This provides for two points of line spacing (separation leading) between adjacent ascenders and descenders. Figure 6-9 also shows this relationship.

Typesetting jargon

6-34. Output Media

Word processing system output can be in the form of hard copy (paper), storage medium (magnetic card, tape, or disk), or micrographic medium (microfilm and microfiche). Paper is still the most common output medium and will be for years to come.

6-35. The Paperless Office, Fact or Fiction? The notion of the "paperless office" is just that, a notion. The fact is that projections are showing an increase in the use of paper. A study conducted for the National Office Products Association of Alexandria, Virginia, forecasted a seven-percent-per-year increase in paper consumption over the next decade for bond, copier, and computer paper.

Paper consumption increasing

This is quite believable, as paper-using output devices are being added to offices by the minute. The addition of paper output devices hints that more and more paper will be generated. Personally, I believe that paper output can be calculated in direct proportion to the available paper-producing capacity!

Paper-handling capacity controls consumption

Having been responsible for all copy equipment in a relatively large business operation, I had the opportunity to test this belief. It was noted that each of three self-service machines was running in the neighborhood of 100,000 copies per month, with an average of three to four people waiting in line at any given time to use these machines. The addition and strategic placement of two more machines was one solution tried, the belief being that this would offer better copy service and curb time being wasted by people walking to and from the machines and waiting in lines to make copies.

The result: instead of having three machines run 100,000 copies per month each, there were five machines running 100,000 copies per month each. The lines still averaged three to four people. Perhaps another moral to the story is embodied in another personal belief: You can't save paper by adding paper output devices.

It didn't work

There are many kinds of paper available for use on word processing systems. Any paper that can be used on a standard typewriter can be used on a word processing system's letter-quality printer. This includes standard bonds of various weights as well as preprinted forms, letterhead stationery, and legal-size stock. In addition to standard sheet stock, continuous-form papers can be used. Paragraph 6-27 describes the use of continuous-form paper.

6-36. Output on Paperless Media. There may be some hope for reducing paper consumption through exclusive document storage on magnetic and micrographic media. Once business people begin to trust magnetic media as reliable, they may simply keep documents filed on disks or tape. However, a major drawback to magnetic archiving is the fear of losing data. Magnetic media can be damaged by magnetic fields, extremes of temperature, and physical mutilation. For this reason, most businesses keep "back-up" files in hard-copy form for insurance.

Magnetic and micrographics media

Micrographic processes are being used more and more as time goes on. Devices such as computer output microfilm (COM) and 35-millimeter reproduction cameras allow documents to be reduced in size and stored on small film strips or rectangular microfiche film. This is an excellent way to archive documents that must be retained for some period of time. Reader equipment, which illuminates, magnifies, and displays a microfilm document on a screen, can be used to read microfilm-filed documents, but the quality is often poor. Some users complain that continuous use of microfilm readers causes eyestrain.

Blow-back quality suffers

Micrographic copier devices are available when hard copy of a reduced document is required. However, the quality of the micrographic blow-back image (re-created from the film image) is rarely as sharp as the original. Micrographics media are best used in applications where compact storage and easy, inexpensive document distribution are desired.

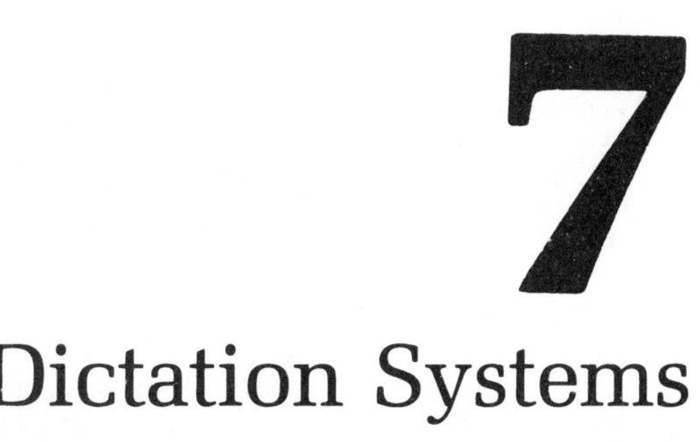

7 Dictation Systems

7-1. INTRODUCTION

Dictation equipment is rapidly replacing shorthand. Although dictation is often overlooked when discussing the benefits and functions of word processing, it is heavily used in many word processing centers. This chapter provides an overview of dictating systems, describing some of the advantages of dictation, preparing people for dictation, types of equipment and systems, and typical uses in word processing environments. We'll refer to the person dictating as the author and the one transcribing the dictation as the transcriptionist.

Replaces shorthand

7-2. ADVANTAGES OF DICTATION

Most businesses that are sensitive to productivity, particularly administrative productivity, encourage the use of dictation equipment for many reasons. First of all, when shorthand is used, two people are spending valuable time. With dictation, just one person is engaged while the other can be doing something productive. Authors can talk faster, stop and

Two people versus one

review notes, and back up and replace material that they aren't satisfied with, and they can do this at home, on an airplane, or in another city, if required.

Speaking faster than writing

Dictation can usually be done at around 150 words per minute, compared to handwriting at between twenty and thirty words per minute. In addition to saving valuable author time, the transcriptionist saves time, too. The U.S. Navy Management Office found that a secretary could transcribe from a machine thirty-three percent faster than from shorthand or longhand. The transcriptionist can control the speed of the dictated material, back up and replay hard to understand passages, change the tone of the voice for comfort and variety, and stop and restart when an interruption occurs.

Dictation encouraged by many companies

Most dictation equipment companies offer dictation training material and provide classes. Many user companies are adopting internal dictation training courses for authors. They encourage professional people to develop dictating skills so they can communicate their thoughts faster and more efficiently. Many can compose material while they are en route to and from work or on a business trip. They capture their thoughts while they are fresh. Most often they use portable tape recorders, or "note takers," for this purpose.

Telephone dictation a handy tool

Some companies have telephone dictation systems. Often, word processing centers make provisions to accommodate dictation over the telephone to enable authors to dictate from almost any part of the world. They can have written correspondence delivered in a matter of hours, or have it ready for their signature and immediate distribution upon return to the office. If designed properly, the systems can operate twenty-four hours a day. They can operate unattended during nonbusiness hours so that authors can call in and dictate information at night or on weekends.

7-3 Moving Toward the Use of Dictation Equipment

Those companies interested in making their professional and managerial personnel more effective recognize the benefits of dictation to the author and spend a great deal of money on equipment and training programs. However, it takes personal commitment and discipline on the part of the individual author. Often businesses find that their dictation equipment sits idle while the authors, who have taken all the dictation training courses, continue to produce text the way they always have.

Personal commitment to learn dictation

There's no question in their minds that dictation improves author productivity. Those who are trained and equipped and then return to longhand will readily admit that dictation is unquestionably superior. Why don't they convert? Why do central systems and the personal recorders go unused? There are several reasons:

1. Dictation means change; change is threatening.
2. Dictation takes training; authors must know how to dictate and understand why.
3. Dictation takes personal commitment before a serious attempt will be made to try it.
4. Dictation takes a considerable amount of author practice time to reach a comfortable competence level.

Reasons for not dictating

Many businesses take dictation a step at a time. They do this by:

1. Starting in one area or department where they can make a minimal investment
2. Structuring their training to meet specific business needs, thereby making the training program more viable

A workable strategy

3. Concentrating encouragement on a specific group, resulting in motivation and improved visibility of program effectiveness
4. Using group results as a success model to encourage other groups.

An approach like this can

1. Minimize your initial investment in equipment and training
2. Ensure that you receive a return on your investment before making further expenditures

Strategic advantages

3. Use positive motivation by applying the "Hawthorne Effect" principle, making members of the selected group feel special
4. Realize a greater yield in office efficiency through an increased percentage of equipment users
5. Develop a model for use in distributing equipment and training to other areas.

7-4. DICTATION SYSTEMS

There are many kinds of dictation equipment, ranging from small, hand-held recorders to sophisticated central dictation networks that accommodate many authors simultaneously. We'll look at personal recorders and transcribers first and then discuss larger systems.

7-5. Personal Recorders

It can be carried

By personal recorders, we mean equipment that is normally carried or operated by a single author. The recorders are not connected to a central system or wired to a transcriber. They are usually self-contained recorder-playback units, most often battery-powered.

7-6. Personal Recorder Types. There are a variety of recorders available on the market today, with a variety of tape types. The three most common tape types are

Three common formats

1. Standard cassette—thirty minutes per side (most common)
2. Microcassette—thirty minutes per side (most common)
3. Minicassette—fifteen minutes per side (most common).

The three different tape formats are shown in Figure 7-1. Many manufacturers are adding capacity to these tapes to increase the recording times. For example, a one-hour-per-side tape is being considered for the microcassette.

The personal recorders, regardless of tape size, normally offer the following features:

1. Record
2. Play

Figure 7-1. Common Tape Formats (Left to right: standard cassette, minicassette, microcassette)

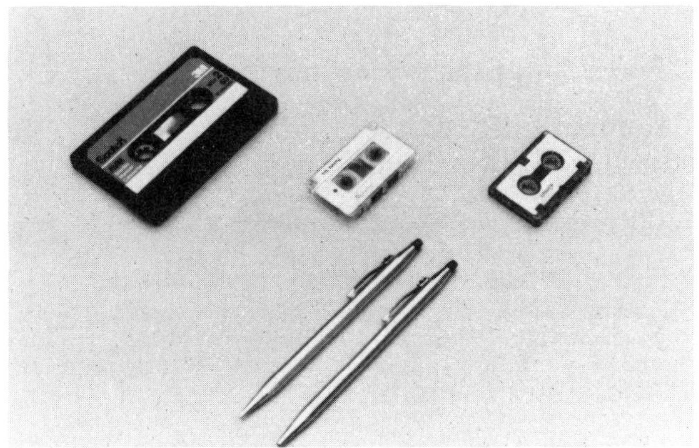

3. Rewind
4. Fast forward
5. Microphone or telephone input jack
6. Speaker output jack
7. Cue (or queue)
8. End of tape warning
9. Tape indexing.

Common features

The first four features are most common. Since all tape recorders are equipped with internal microphones and speakers, some recorders don't accommodate external microphones or speakers. However, there are times when external microphone and speaker jacks can be important. For example, the microphone input can be used to record a telephone conversation by using a telephone pickup loop. The speaker output can be used to couple the audio output of the tape recorder through a phone coupler so that prerecorded information can be played over the telephone.

Some uses

When selecting a personal tape recorder, there are several factors to consider. These include

1. Size and weight
2. Recording capacity or length
3. Compatibility with other recorders and transcription equipment
4. Battery life and rechargeability
5. Alternate power sources
6. Sensitivity
7. Audio output quality
8. User functionality

Important considerations

9. Accessory selection
10. Serviceability.

Let's look at each of these features briefly.

7-7. Size and Weight. The importance of tape recorder size and weight depends on how it will be carried, how it will be used, and how important the audio output quality is. If the unit will be carried in a pocket, a microcassette unit is most likely desirable, although some standard cassette units have been miniaturized extensively. If the author is going to use the unit as a hand-held note-taker, then the microcassette unit is probably the best choice. If the unit can be carried in a briefcase or used on a table top for conference recording, then a larger portable recorder may be desirable. Very small units normally have audio output quality limitations, discussed in paragraph 7-13.

It should be easy to carry

7-8. Recording Capacity or Length. Fifteen minutes per side may be satisfactory for a hand-held note-taker, and in fact most often is. However, if you plan to dictate long passages or record lengthy conversations or conferences, you may need a longer recording capacity. It's certainly inconvenient to interrupt a productive process to change or flip a tape. It can be disastrous to have a tape run to the end and miss important passages of information. Many recorders have built-in warning indicators to let you know when the tape has reached the end. A warning tone or "beep" is usually triggered by the unit when the tape reaches the end of its reel and becomes tight. This is an important feature and should be checked when purchasing a recorder.

Does it record long enough?

7-9. Compatibility. It can be frustrating to have recorded tape that doesn't fit anyone's transcriber. It can also be a problem to acquire a tape format that isn't used by anyone else. It is important to ensure that your portable recorder uses tape that is compatible with other equipment in your company. If there are no other tape recorders, it may still be a good idea to consider what the probability is of other people's getting the same type of equipment. It may mean establishing a policy. Use a standard format. If everyone is using standard cassettes and you decide to use a microcassette, it may work out well as long as you buy a microcassette adapter for the standard cassette transcribers. But check before it's too late. Not all standard cassette transcribers can be adapted for microcassettes.

Be sure it can be used

Another compatibility consideration is the use of accessories. For example, if your equipment is compatible with other equipment, you will be able to share accessories such as microphones, telephone pickup loops, and tape erasers.

7-10. Battery Life and Rechargeability. The portable power source for personal-size tape recorders is an important consideration. How long will the recorder operate on a set of batteries? If the unit uses standard alkaline throw-away batteries, are they the 9-volt transistor type or 1.2-volt AA cells? The transistor type batteries will provide significantly longer service. However, if the units are rechargeable, the rechargeable nickel-cadmium AA cells will probably be satisfactory. Some units have internal recharging circuits which allow recharging without removing the batteries. Others have separate battery-charging units. The separate units make it necessary to remove the batteries from the tape recorder for recharging. Whatever type of recorder you select, it is always a good idea to carry extra batteries in case the ones in the unit run down. In addition, your recorder should use batteries that are easily obtainable at convenience or drug stores.

The power source is important

7-11. Alternate Power Sources. Some portable recorders have power cords which allow them to be plugged into a standard AC wall outlet. Others have AC adapters which plug into an AC wall outlet and connect to a power jack on the recorder unit. In either case, it is always a good idea to have an alternate power source available in the event that you use up your battery supply. It may even be a good idea to keep the alternate source handy when traveling just in case it is needed. When traveling abroad, it's wise to carry a regulated power converter suitable for motor-speed control and a plug adapter unit. These can be obtained at electronic supply outlets such as Radio Shack.

Carry a back-up source when you travel

7-12. Sensitivity. The sensitivity of a tape recorder usually refers to its ability to detect different noise levels. Most units have automatic gain control (AGC) circuits which amplify soft sounds and suppress excessively loud ones. It can be important to suppress background noise to prevent interference with the author's dictation. It is always a good idea to test a tape recorder's sensitivity to see if it can pick up the intelligence being recorded. For example, you might want to set it in the middle of a table and conduct a conversation. Have a trial run, then listen to it to see if it picked up everything clearly. Also, you'll want to set how loud background noise is to see if the interference is sufficiently loud to make transcribing uncomfortable.

Know what it can do

7-13. Audio Output Quality. When audio output quality is important, a very small tape recorder may not do the job. Compact speakers cannot provide the full response range and corresponding quality of a large speaker. In addition, the audio output circuits are more compact and don't provide the reproduction quality or volume normally necessary for a large room. However, if the tape can be moved from a small

Be sure it's loud and clear

recorder to a larger one with good audio reproduction quality, you'll often find that even the smallest microcassette units have excellent audio recording quality. If one unit will be used for both recording and playback, a larger unit may be preferable.

7-14. User Functionality. There are many different recorders, with as many different sets of controls and indicators. The important thing, in terms of functionality, is to select a unit that is simple to operate and that the user feels comfortable with. If it takes two hands to manipulate the various functions, then the unit is probably not well designed. If you can control record, playback, rewind, and fast forward with a thumb or finger, and the motions seem natural, then the unit is probably functionally packaged and may be suitable. You should also be able to look at the unit to determine whether or not it is recording properly during operation. It can be quite costly to discover that the unit didn't record material after the author has completed a lengthy passage of dictation.

Is it easy to use?

There are times when fast playback is desirable. For example, the author may wish to telephone recorded passages long-distance to a recording transcriber or central dictation system at the office. If this is the case, playback in fast forward can save a significant amount of time as well as reduce the telephone charges.

Some recorders are equipped to speed up playback for this purpose. When looking for this feature, be sure that the playback is at a constant speed so that the transcriptionist doesn't have to "chase" the information by varying the transcriber speed control. Also, you must be certain that the transcriber has the speed control range necessary to slow down the playback to a comfortable transcription rate.

Fast playback can be a handy feature

Figure 7-2. A Microcassette Recorder and Accessories (Recorder at center. Clockwise: cassettes, power source, batteries, telephone adapter)

7-15. Accessory Selection. When choosing a recorder, you will always be interested in the accessories available. The manufacturer's brochures and catalogs can be reviewed to compare the array of equipment and accessories. Even though you may be solving a simple dictation job in the beginning, you may discover more and more uses for the dictating equipment as your familiarity with it increases. You may want to couple transcribers to the telephone for recording phone messages, or tie one transcriber into two remote dictation units. Whatever the case, look at competing equipment information and see if the equipment you are considering is upgradable. Figure 7-2 shows a microcassette recorder and some available accessories.

Check those accessories

7-16. Serviceability. It is always important to have a service organization behind the equipment you buy. If it becomes defective and you can't get it repaired, you'll have to purchase another unit. Some manufacturers sell service contracts; others have repair centers that charge a nominal fee for repair. Whichever method you choose, be sure that your unit can be repaired promptly by qualified repair personnel.

Figure 7-3. A Recorder-Transcriber Combination Unit (Microphone at Center. Clockwise: cassette, foot control, headset, recorder-transcriber)

7-17 Desk-Top Transcribers

This section discusses desk-top transcribers. Large, central system transcribers will be covered in paragraph 7-23.

Lots to choose from

There are almost as many transcribers available on the market as there are tape recorders. In fact, some units double as tape recorders and transcribers. Such a unit is shown in Figure 7-3. When selecting a transcriber, there are several factors that should be considered, just as in the selection of recorders. These include

Important considerations

1. Document searching (or indexing)
2. Speed control and speech quality
3. Functionality
4. Accessories
5. Serviceability.

7-18. Document Searching. Document searching is commonly done in three ways:

1. Digital location indicators
2. Paper marking strips
3. Tape cueing (or queueing).

Digital locating indicators are numerical reference wheels that indicate relative locations on the tape. These wheels are normally "zeroed" at the beginning of a tape, or when the tape is fully rewound. The transcriptionist must note the numerical display at the beginning of each recorded document. For example, the first document might begin at location 000 and end at 089; the second might begin at 090 and end at 215. By writing the numbers down on a note pad, the transcriptionist can advance or rewind to the beginning of documents by referring to the digital indicator.

An old but simple system

Paper marking strips work much in the same way as a digital locating indicator and note pad, except that the note pad is built into the transcriber. This eliminates the need for writing things down on a separate piece of paper. This sytem requires the transcriptionist to install a paper marking strip on the transcriber when a new tape is installed. A pointer moves across the strip as the tape advances. When the end of a document is reached, the transcriptionist presses a lever or button which marks the paper strip. When the tape is removed, the strip can be stored with the tape for future reference.

Document indication

Tape cueing is done either by putting intelligence on the tape with a "cue" button located on the tape recorder or automatically by the recorder prior to each document. Transcribers equipped to detect cues will automatically fast-forward the tape to cue locations. This lets the machine locate the beginning of new documents automatically or advance to some point where the author has dictated a note. For example, an author might have afterthoughts upon

Special notes

completing a document and decide to leave some special instructions for changes. The transcriber will automatically advance to the cue and the transcriptionist can listen to the special instructions before proceeding with the transcribing task.

7-19. Speed Control and Speech Quality. Speed control is normally used to slow down a fast-talking author so that the transcriptionist can keep up. It can also be used to speed up a slow-talking author. When the speed is reduced, the frequency or tone of the voice becomes lower on most transcribers. Conversely, the tone becomes higher when the transcriber is sped up. There are some transcribers that have built-in tone compensation circuits that hold the tone at the same level, regardless of the speed.

Check out the speed control range

Most transcribers allow approximately twenty percent speed variation; however, there are some that allow significantly greater variation. The units with greater speed range can be used to slow down fast-forward playback by authors who use time-saving speech compression methods similar to that described in paragraph 7-14.

7-20. Functionality. Most transcribers are quite functional and easy to use. All have instruction manuals that describe controls and indicators and provide operating instructions. The transcriber should be light enough to be moved easily, have a good tape indexing system, have provisions for telephone and remote control connection, and if required, double as a recorder.

Many double as recorders

Many have speakers; those without speakers require earphones for output. If a speaker is not needed, then a speakerless model may be adequate. Many standard cassette units have minicassette and microcassette adapters. If the transcriber will be used with various kinds of cassettes, it is important that the adapters be easy to install and remove.

Tape controls, such as fast forward and rewind, should be simple and positive. If you have to hold a button down for fast-forward or rewind instead of simply setting a control and having the machine do the tape winding unattended, the machine might not be for you. Look at the machine's functionality carefully before making a final selection.

Keep it simple

7-21. Accessories. Available transcriber accessories should be examined carefully. Some business applications may gain by having a transcriber that can serve double duty. If it has microphones, telephone input units, foot control, document searching, and various cassette type adapters, and it is compatible with the portable units already being used, then it's probably a good choice. Just like other office equipment, it should be upgradable, even if you don't initially plan to use all of the available features.

Some do it all

7-22. Serviceability. Service considerations for transcribers are the same as those mentioned for recorders in paragraph 7-16. The integrity of the manufacturer and the availability of qualified service personnel are important. Something that is often done is to ask the salesman for a list of customers who are using his product. Call them and see how they feel about the reliability of the unit and the kind of service they are receiving. If they are satisfied, you can have good expectations. If they are dissatisfied, you'd better look at another brand of dictation equipment.

Check the service

7-23 Central Dictation Systems

Central dictation systems are normally installed in business activities where it is desirable for a number of authors to share a sophisticated dictation equipment resource. Dictation systems of this type are normally located in dictation or word processing centers where transcription can be accomplished on automatic word processing equipment.

Many kinds to choose from

There are several kinds of central dictation systems. They vary in complexity and features. In fact, a cluster of standard desk-top transcribers can make up a central system in the simplest sense. More complex central dictation systems have work distribution panels, supervisor intercoms, backlog measurement devices, and other features for identifying, distributing, and measuring work in progress.

Remote control by telephone

7-24. Author Input. Most central systems can be reached by telephone. When an author wishes to dictate by telephone, he can dial a number that provides access to the dictation system. Once he has *seized* (gained access to) the system, he uses digits on the telephone to control the central system functions. Table 7-1 contains a list of one manufacturer's recorder control code.

Table 7-1. Typical Recorder Control Code for Remote Telephone Access

Digit	Function	Description
1	Hold/Restart	Stops or restarts dictation unit for long pauses or interruptions.
2	Stop/Correct	Stops playback to permit corrections. Also stops fast rewind or fast forward when scanning dictation.
3	Review	Permits review of last few words of dictation.
4	Fast forward	Fast forward to end of dictation.
5	Manual disconnect	Required if system is not provided with automatic disconnect on hang-up.
6	Access	Permits access to auxiliary recorder for priority dictation, confidential memos, telexes, or special messages.
7	Fast rewind	Fast rewind to beginning of dictation with automatic playback.
0	Supervisor call	Permits direct communication with transcription supervisor.

7-25. Number of System Dictation Channels. By dictation channels, we mean the number of input lines that can simultaneously be used by authors. In central systems, a recorder is required for each author. The number of channels required depends entirely on the number of authors and the amount of time they dictate on the system. Most systems are modularly expandable. You can start with a small number of channels and grow with the requirements as demand increases.

Most can be upgraded

7-26. Types of Central Recorders. Central system recorders can be cassette-type or continuous-loop *tank*-type units. The cassette type normally records thirty minutes per cassette. Once the cassette is full or is recorded to a preselected percentage or number of minutes, it ejects into a tray. Ejected cassettes are in line for transcription. Upon ejection, a fresh cassette is put in place for further dictation. The change cycle takes anywhere from eight to twelve seconds. The unit normally emits a tone during the change to alert the author to stop dictation momentarily. Once a new tape is in place, the tone stops and the author can continue dictation.

Tanks and cassettes

Tank recorders range from two to four hours of continuous dictation. These systems are connected to work distribution panels that switch the dictation to desk-top transcribers, connected to the distribution panel by cables. When the tank is full, it can be *bled off* (unloaded onto cassettes) to free it for further dictation.

7-27. Work Distribution Panels. Work distribution panels are used primarily with tank systems. They are usually modularly upgradable; that is, you can start with one or two channels and add more as the demand increases. The panels usually have provisions for supervisor intercom, either to authors or transcriptionists, dictation backlog measurement,

Distribution of workload possible

and transcriber selection for balancing the transcription workload. The panels also show dictation status, that is, whether an author is presently using or has recently accessed the unit, and have indicators that call attention to priority transcription requirements.

Additional features, such as work measurement; hard copy indication; prerecorded author instructions; automatic cassette labeling with author identification, date, and time information; time-in/time-out data for charge-out computation; and others are being heavily marketed on many systems.

Monitor systems tell the story

Monitor systems with CRT displays are often used to measure dictation backlog, work in progress, and work completed. When used with cassette-based systems, each tape cassette is processed through a monitoring device or reader which records time and author identification information contained on the tape. The information is coded on the tape when authors enter their recorder control codes by telephone. The central system has an internal clock which enters time and date information. Once the information is read from the tape cassettes to the monitor system, the dictation center supervisor can review dictation transactions on the monitor screen. If desired, the transactions can be filed on a chart to provide a permanent record.

The cassette systems appear to be more popular since standard cassettes fit both central systems and personal recorders. Another reason many people prefer cassette-based systems is that they enable expanded work distribution simply by carrying cassettes to work stations equipped with standard cassette transcribers. The tank systems are hard-wired to the transcription stations. However, tanks can be rerecorded on standard cassettes in order to redistribute the transcription workload.

7-28. Typical Central System. Figure 7-4 is a diagram of a large central dictation system. A description of

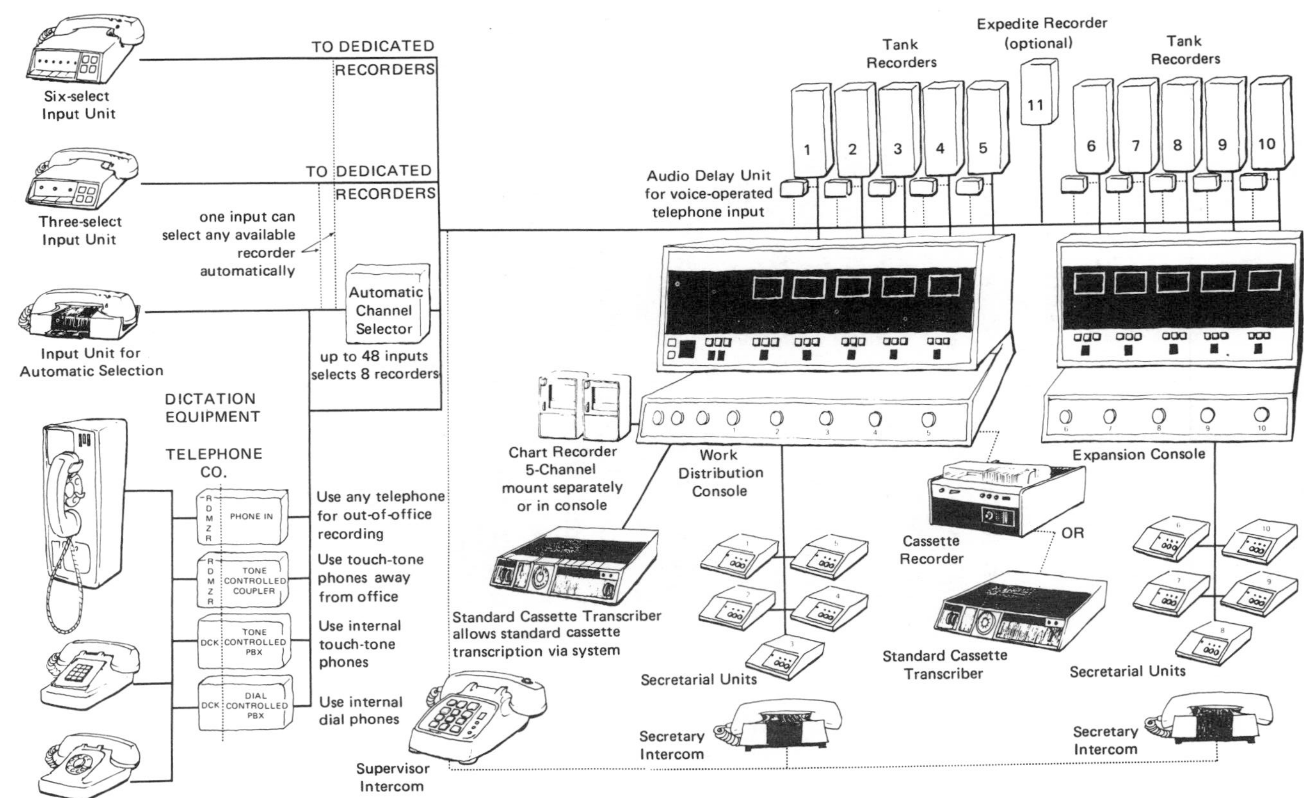

Figure 7-4. Central Dictation System Component Identification and Equipment Relationships

the system is provided for a better understanding of the parts of the system and how they relate to each other.

How a big system works

Figure 7-4 illustrates an eleven-channel tank recorder system that employs a work distribution console and a variety of input and output devices. The automatic channel selector, if used, allows up to forty-eight inputs and can select any eight of the ten recorders. Recorders are selected according to availabiity. When a recorder is filled to capacity, it is not selected by the automatic channel selector.

Lots of input devices

The input devices include hard-wired six-select and three-select units which allow an author to select any one of six (or three) specific recorders without going through the automatic channel selector. If required, these units can use one channel for access to the automatic channel selector, allowing them to select any available recorder in the system. These input units are normally located in the same building as the central dictation system, since they are connected by cable. The other input units, including the unit for automatic selection and standard internal and external telephones, can be routed through the automatic channel selector.

Telephone input

Telephone instruments often serve authors as dictation devices. Note that the diagram shows dial phones and touch-tone phones and a variety of interface devices for coupling these instruments to the system. This allows authors to use telephones in their office, at home, or even when they are out of the city on business trips.

As mentioned earlier in this chapter, authors can control the recorder by using different digits on their phone during dictation. Table 7-1 lists one manufacturer's recorder control code system.

The system illustrated has eleven continuous-loop tank recorders. Ten of the recorders are equipped with audio delay units, while the eleventh, which is used for priority dictation, does not use an audio delay unit. The delay units control the recorders when they are in use. If an author stops dictating, the audio delay units stop the tape advance until the author resumes dictation. Upon resumption, the audio delay units restart the recorders. This feature conserves tape during long pauses and eliminates long dictation voids for the transcriptionist.

Delay units save tape

Each of the recorder outputs is connected to the work distribution console, which is capable of distributing recorded material to one of ten desk-top secretarial units or to a cassette recorder. Recorders 1 through 5 can be connected to any of secretarial units 1 through 5 by means of a switch on the front panel of the console. Some work distribution consoles use plugs and jacks, similar to a telephone switchboard, for work distribution.

Distribution balances the load

The standard cassette transcriber unit is used for inputting standard cassette transcription to the system. For example, if an author dictates material on a standard cassette or portable microcassette recorder, he or she can give it to the dictation center, where it can be put on the standard cassette transcriber for input to the system. The work distribution console can switch the material to one of the secretarial units for transcription.

Provisions for standard cassettes

The cassette recorder is used to rerecord, or "bleed," material from the tank recorders during peak dictation backlog to provide expanded capacity in the tank recorders. For example, if they are full, dictation can be bled to standard cassettes. Once the dictation is transferred, the tanks are free to record additional information. Another advantage of the cassette recorder unit is that it accommodates increased distribution of the transcription load. Standard cassette transcriber units can be used to process the work in parallel with the dedicated secretarial units.

Cassettes increase work distribution

This system also has a supervisor intercom unit and secretary intercom units. These allow the dictation supervisor to have direct communication with the transcriptionists in order to discuss workloads and priorities.

The chart recorders, which can be mounted separately or directly on the work distribution console, are used to record dictation backlog and transcription. Devices like these can be used to measure workloads and material processed and indicate peak periods; they can be valuable for analysis of dictation activity.

7-29. Other Systems. Many central systems use cassette recorders instead of tank recorders. The work distribution is done manually by simply handing recorded cassettes to transcriptionists equipped with standard cassette transcribers. Many central cassette systems are equipped with workload monitors, labeling devices, and other features. With these features, the system measures backlog, identifies authors, records the hour and minute that dictation was started and stopped, and indicates priority transcription work.

Work load monitors

8 Analyzing Business Needs

8-1. INTRODUCTION

Tips on analysis

This chapter provides some tips on how to analyze present business operations. Once you know what's being done, you can better determine what's needed to streamline office transactions and increase overall performance. Some of the principles described can be used in areas other than the office. In fact, they can be applied directly to manufacturing warehousing, data processing, and other operations in your business.

8-2. AN APPROACH TO SYSTEM ANALYSIS

The adoption of a simple checklist is a good place to start preparing your analysis of a business operation. Entries should include

1. Adopting an objective attitude
2. Developing an understanding of the overall operation before looking at individual process steps as candidates for improvement

3. Developing an understanding of modeling principles (zero-base budgeting)
4. Determining what your present operation is costing the business
5. Challenging every operation
6. Determining alternative processes
7. Testing and documenting results
8. Selling the solution to top management
9. Installing changes
10. Monitoring performance through models.

A simple checklist

8-3. Objectivity

Objectivity is an essential part of good analysis. Your attitude must be as free from biases toward system types, manufacturers, preconceived organizational structures, and internal emotional pressures as possible. Such biases often contribute to poor decisions. Decisions based on internal emotional pressures possibly rate the worst. Many word processing system sales representatives will admit that a large percentage of their sales or leases are founded upon emotion. Not that the systems don't contribute to improved performance. But the real reason for selection might be completely wrong. One such instance of this might be as follows:

Don't let emotion decide

> Manager A acquires a new word processing system for his area. Managers B and C take note of Manager A's new acquisition. Manager B, not to be outdone, decides to follow suit. If Manager A has a new word processing system and she doesn't, her status could be impaired. This is a simple case of "keeping up with the Joneses."
>
> Manager C begins to get pressure from members of his staff. "If Manager A's people have got one, why can't we get one, too?" This is an outright form of coercion that a strong manager wouldn't tolerate. But Manager C isn't strong, and to keep from losing face

An unhappy story

with his people, he decides to look for the necessary funding. Within a month after Manager A's system installation, Managers B and C fall in line with requests for capital.

These are not reasons for making a $10,000 to $30,000 capital investment. There's only one reason for this kind of an investment in any business: a bona fide business need. If an investment can't readily pay for itself in dollars and cents, it shouldn't be made. Before making the investment, be sure you've checked the alternatives from a completely objective point of view. Don't get caught in the trap of *backing in* (make a preconceived set of numbers seem rational) to a set of cost justification numbers to support a decision you've already made. Develop your numbers from the bottom up. When this is done, you'll know why the investment is being made, and you'll also wind up with a system that fits your business activity.

Don't back into numbers

8-4. Understand the Overall Operation

Next, you should develop a good understanding of the overall operation, knowing why things are done, how they interrelate, even how they got started. Managers who zero in on single processes before seeing the big picture can make costly assumptions. It's the system that's important, not a single step in the process. By understanding present barriers to system performance in an operation, things can often be improved without spending a dime on new equipment. In fact, adding sophisticated equipment isn't always an automatic route to improved performance.

You can improve without spending a dime

8-5. Modeling

Once the system is understood, an excellent approach is to develop a sound *business model*. A knowledge of business modeling will help you in getting a handle on number 4 of the checklist, what your present operation is costing the business. Once this is known, things will begin to fall into place.

8-6. Using Models for Measuring Performance. Modeling is an effective management tool that has been used for a number of years. It measures performance and encourages the attainment of goals. Business models determine theoretically attainable performance levels and can therefore be used to evaluate the efficiency of your present operation. Some fundamental objectives of modeling include

A vigorous business discipline

1. Evaluating what is happening relative to what should be happening
2. Providing a basis for performance goals
3. Identifying areas for improvement
4. Providing a basis for cost reduction
5. Detecting major business forecast errors
6. Testing basic cost assumptions of a business operation.

Some modeling objectives

Models are simply lists of performance standards for a business operation. Thorough models include measurement indices for all major process points within an operation. Once present performance standards are determined, they must be communicated to everyone in the operation. By knowing what is expected, your people can achieve model performance levels. Models can and should be used as an incentive for improved performance in cost reduction, productivity, quality, scrap reduction, material consumption, and overhead expense.

8-7. Modeling versus Trending (Zero-Base Budgeting). Trending is used by many businesses to determine what expenditures can be expected in future accounting periods. Trending is based on what has been happening; it uses historical information to establish future business objectives. This means that trending states what the business *has been doing;* modeling, on the other hand, states what the business *should be doing.* The true modeling approach to management is actually a form of *zero-base budgeting.* Simply stated, zero-base budgeting discounts what has happened in the past and takes a look at the business from the ground up. It challenges every element of the business to determine the lowest achievable cost, fastest achievable cycle time, highest achievable quality, or other measurable standard. Only by reviewing all the supporting details can unnecessary activities and expenditures be eliminated. This puts an end to doing things because "that's the way we've always done it." The zero-base approach has proven to be an excellent business discipline which results in ambitious and achievable goals.

What's been versus what should be

Models are normally developed in conjunction with the people who use them or are responsible for making them happen. The natural tendency to improve, coupled to models, which are statements of what should be achieved in a particular time, makes modeling a viable business thrust. When all levels of people are involved in model development, communication is maximized, actions required to meet model performance are clear, and achievement becomes a matter of pride.

Achievement a matter of pride

By continually comparing actual performance to model expectations from period to period, models are tested for realism. Regularly scheduled review activity ensures that models as well as corresponding performance continue to improve. Once models are well established, forecasts don't have to be continually inspected. All that has to be reviewed is the difference between model performance and actual performance.

Management by exception

8-8. Determine Present Business Costs

It may be quite easy to determine the cost of a business operation simply by looking at accounting records. Many businesses use a cost-collection system based on discrete business entities. When this is the case, items like materials, labor, overhead, space, utilities, equipment depreciation and leases, and other direct costs are easy to retrieve. If the business doesn't have a sophisticated cost-collection system, these costs have to be calculated manually.

Develop a financial picture

8-9. Isolating Costs of Specific Steps. Even with sophisticated cost-collection systems, it is often necessary to isolate the cost of specific steps or processes manually. This is frequently the only way to determine what certain activities are worth to the business. When determining specific process costs, you'll want to understand standard model costs in terms such as

Typical model indices

- net units produced per direct labor hour
- keystrokes per hour
- minutes per office transaction (specific type)
- supply cost per net unit produced
- supply volume consumed per process
- scrap value as a percent of total material cost
- equipment depreciation or lease as a percent of product value
- equipment downtime
- number of items processed per square foot of space
- number of sales dollars generated per person
- payroll as a percent of sales dollars
- material or supplies as a percent of sales dollars
- inventory cost as a percent of billable activity
- profit after taxes as a percent of business assets
- direct labor hours per page unit

- indirect labor hours per direct labor hour
- attendance hours as a percent of available work hours
- and more.

All of these standards can be used as indices for business models.

8-10. Using Model Indices. In the preparation of a documentation page, specific model indices might include:

List of Model Indices for Document Page Preparation	Standard
Number of hours per written page unit (including research)	3.7 hr.
Number of hours per line illustration unit (including checking)	2.8 hr.
Number of hours per tone illustration unit (including checking)	1.6 hr.
Number of minutes per typed draft page unit	12.0 min.
Number of minutes per edited draft page unit	8.0 min.
Number of minutes per author reviewed page unit	9.0 min.
Number of minutes per final page unit composition	18.2 min.
Number of minutes per final illustration page composition	4.0 min.
Number of minutes per page unit makeup	3.8 min.
Number of minutes per proofread page	5.8 min.
Number of minutes per final page check/document assembly	3.0 min.

Conversion to Standard Units. Notice that illustration units and page units are used as a standard. It is necessary to convert data into uniform units of measure in order to get an "apples-to-apples" comparison. Some examples of conversion to a common unit for measurement purposes can be as follows:

Convert to the standard

One page unit is an equivalent 8½-by-11-inch single-spaced page using twelve-pitch or ten-point proportional-space type, with a column width of seven inches and a page depth of nine inches. To convert nonstandard pages to standard page units, the following factors are used:

Double-spaced twelve-pitch draft page:
multiply by 0.5

Double-spaced ten-pitch draft page:
multiply by 0.42

Single-spaced handwritten manuscript page:
multiply by 0.67

Double-spaced handwritten manuscript page:
multiply by 0.33

Judgment must be used to factor standard multipliers on handwritten material. For example, if an author writes smaller than average, the factor would be increased.

A line illustration unit (one that is made up of drawn lines) is a seven-by-nine-inch image area with nominal line density. Judgment must be used for complex or simple drawings. To convert a drawing size of 15½ inches by nine-inches to a standard line illustration unit, a multiplier of 2.0 would be used.

Using Indices to Measure Performance. Model indices provide measurable evidence of performance. Performance of the organization as well as individual performance can be measured. Both supervisors and individual contributors know what is expected. It's easy to quantify the capabilities of each of your peo-

Indices provide quantitative evidence

ple. Everyone knows what kind of a job they are doing relative to the model.

Using Indices for Resource Planning. A major advantage of having a business model is that it helps to plan work. For example, if a large business backlog is forecast, knowing what resources are required to perform a given number of business transactions within a specific period of time becomes a relatively simple calculation. Using the above model indices as standards, and knowing the manuscript of a 240-page proposal with 86 illustration units (68 line and 18 tone) is forecast for editing, composition, and illustrating, you can compute your labor requirements as follows:

Indices help plan backlog

Applying indices to scheduling

Editing:	240 pp. × (8.0 + 3.0)min/p. = 2640 min. ÷ 60 min./hr.	=	44 hr.
Illustrating:	68 line illus. units × 2.8 hr./unit	=	190 hr.
	18 tone illus. units × 1.2 hr./unit	=	22 hr.
Total illustrating time:			212 hr.
Composition:	240 p. units × 45.8 min./p. = 10,992 min. ÷ 60 min./hr.	=	183 hr.
	86 illus. units × 4.0 min./unit = 344 min. ÷ 60 min./hr.	=	6 hr.
Total composition time:			189 hr.

Using Indices for Cost Estimating. An outstanding benefit of having a good set of business indices is that they are extremely helpful in cost estimating. Not only can you determine the cost of your business operation, but you can also use the indices as multipliers when figuring job cost. For instance, the cost of the above 240-page proposal can be quickly estimated by using labor, material, and overhead rates.

Cost estimating made easy

8-11. Collecting Data. There are many ways to collect information. A common approach is to develop work sheets to be used by people in the operation. It is imperative that each person understand the intent and use of work sheets. They are not used to measure individual performance during the collection period, but instead, to establish process performance. People are not being compared during standard development. Only averages are being computed. This is an extremely difficult concept to get across. However, to gather the data efficiently, you'll either have to stand at the input and output end of a process with a stopwatch and clipboard, which may scare everyone to death, or get your people involved. If they see that you're interested in helping them find easier ways to accomplish their jobs, they may pitch in willingly. In fact, if they perceive the monitoring function as an opportunity to demonstrate their administrative capabilities, they may welcome the responsibility.

Show them why

In addition to selling people on the idea of helping to collect data, the work sheets must be well designed and easy to fill out. This is important for several reasons. First, you don't want your people wasting a lot of time on paperwork. Not only is this time-consuming, but it will also skew your data. Things will tend to take longer than they ordinarily would without data collection. Secondly, if the work sheets are too complex, the accuracy of the information you get back may be in jeopardy. People may not understand what is wanted on the work sheets, and consequently they may write down the wrong kind of information. Thirdly, the information recorded must be meaningful. Finally, it should be easy to tabulate.

Make it easy and meaningful

8-12. Challenge Every Step

Once you understand operation costs and have data that tell you what's presently happening, you're ready for the next step in the process: challenge every step. By using a model approach to the business operation being analyzed, you should be able to break the business system down into functional process steps. It's easy to get side-tracked here. Often the natural tendency is to look at the organizational entities as functional steps. For example, an organization may have sections named:

Break the business down into small pieces

- Administrative Support
- Customer Service
- Data Collection
- Correspondence Services
- Reproduction and Copying Services
- Communication Services

Organizational entities

These are organizational areas, not functional areas. A list of functional steps that are typically required to generate a document include:

1. Originate document
2. Type draft
3. Review document
4. Incorporate comments
5. Review final document
6. Reproduce document
7. Distribute document
8. Store document masters.

Functional entities

Within each of these functional steps, there are often substeps. Figure 8-1 shows the flow of the reproduction, distribution, and storage functions and alternatives that are common to many operations.

Once the functions are identified and flow-charted, each step in the process can be listed; once steps are isolated and listed, alternatives to steps and groups of steps can be studied. Looking at a single step is not as helpful as looking at groups of steps. What's done in the prior step? What's done in the next one? Can several steps be combined? Will this eliminate unnecessary movement? This is where the challenge process starts. Challenging every step includes answering the following questions.

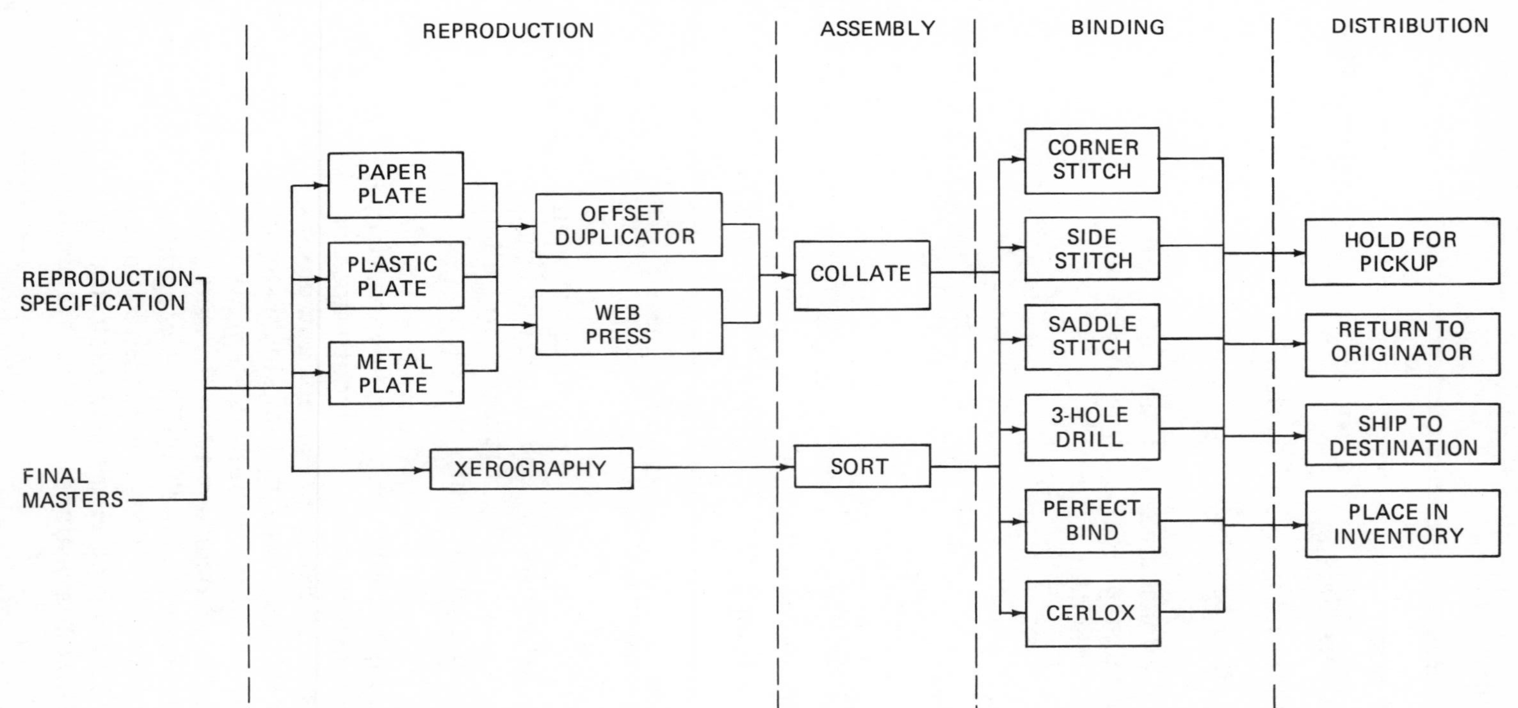

Figure 8-1. Flow-Charting Functional Operations

1. What is being done?
2. Why is it done?
3. Where is it done?
4. When is it done?
5. Who does it?
6. Why do they do it?
7. Can it be done somewhere else?
8. Can it be eliminated?

Ask these questions

Only after these questions are answered are you ready to move to the next entry on your checklist.

8-13. Determine Alternative Processes

This is the creative portion of your analysis. In fact, when done objectively, you may find that what seemed to be a logical organization didn't match functional flow at all. You may find that several functions are almost identical. The people involved have similar skill levels and use common equipment. Can the two process areas be combined? What are the advantages? You may save space and equipment costs and even reduce staffing levels. What are the disadvantages? If the processes work at different paces—for example, one a quick-reaction shop and the other a long-term scheduled production service—they may be incompatible. When you have the answers, you may be ready to draw a new flow chart of your operation to determine if restructuring is an efficient answer to increased business performance.

Alternatives may be obvious

If you look to office automation as an alternative, it's essential to keep the entire business system in mind. Of course, you'll want to zero in on those areas considered cost "hot spots," where you can save big bucks by making process changes. However, the impact on everything from the front of the system to

Prioritize the costs

the back must be carefully analyzed. If you restrict thinking to automation of a single process step, you'll find the preceding process steps unable to keep pace with the automated one, and downstream processes will become bottlenecks.

In determining alternative processes, particularly automated ones, you'll be required to look at a number of different kinds of equipment. A good practice is to look at operations similar to your own for ideas of what's being done in your industry. Of course, it's always more fun to be an innovator, and there are those who don't think anyone else can help. This is sometimes called the "not invented here (NIH) syndrome." Don't fall prey to NIH; there are just too many smart people with good ideas to ignore. It's valuable to see what others are doing. Most business managers are proud of new, high-technology processes and are anxious to share information about their successes with you. If you're lucky, they may share information about their failures as well. Their positive results may give you some good ideas, and you may be able to learn some valuable lessons from the other guy's failures also. This approach to evaluating alternative processes is basically looking at business operations that have found some keys to efficiency and increased performance and using these as success models for your own operation. Some guidelines to system selection are provided in Chapter 9.

Look at other operations for ideas

8-14. Test and Document Results

Once your alternatives have been selected, you'll have to test your assumptions through modeling. Knowing what your business is presently doing in terms of cost and performance is the first step. By putting the new business system on paper, whether it is simply a restructuring, the addition of office automation, or a combination of restructuring and automation, you'll have to determine the impact of

Quantify the impact

the changes in quantitative terms. The more indices you record, the better prepared you'll be for the presentation step. The indices may be stated in the terms listed in paragraph 8-9.

Common improvements involve increased transactions per hour, increased product quality, and reductions in process cycle time. Your projections should be conservative. This is particularly important for automated equipment projections, where theoretical equipment performance and real performance can vary widely. For example, a printer that runs at forty characters per second may be limited by an operator who performs keyboard work at seventy words per minute (six characters per second). The printer will be idle most of the time. In addition, the operator speed of seventy words per minute is also greatly overstated. Actual keyboard speed may only be thirty-five words per minute (three characters per second). Operators take breaks, talk on the phone, sometimes return late from lunch, talk with other nearby operators, are absent due to illness, and take vacations. They also experience learning curves and machine down-time, which are also barriers to attainment of theoretical performance. It's important to comprehend all these things when converting theoretical performance to effective performance.

Theoretical versus effective performance

8-15. Sell the Solution to Top Management

Honesty is the only policy to use in developing your plan and documenting its impact on performance. Don't let yourself be fooled by the claims of automatic equipment manufacturers. Check them out. Above all, don't inadvertently fool the boss. Credibility is one of the most important assets a business manager can have. If you misrepresent the facts, you may never get your boss to believe you again.

The documentation you present should be highly quantitative. This is where your model is helpful.

Specific model indices can be compared to show how the new system is superior to the present one. Showing a comparison sheet of existing system standards and proposed system standards is always a good practice. The improvement in performance should offer payback. The faster a system pays for itself, the better. This is particularly true in periods of high interest.

Show quantitative facts

It's also good to have alternative system information as back-up to your presentation to show you've investigated a number of approaches. A lot of presentations fail when the presenter is asked to go check on other approaches. If this has already been done, the reviewing manager will have confidence in both you and your material and be more likely to approve your request.

Have alternatives ready

8-16. Install Changes

The way a new business system is installed, regardless of the type, is key to its success. It's important to ensure that all bases are covered when bringing a new system on line. This includes developing a thorough schedule that comprehends

Installation planning

1. Preparing the people involved through
   a. Meetings
   b. Participation in analysis
   c. Training
2. Ordering supplies in accordance with delivery lead times
3. Preparing facilities
   a. Furniture and fixture procurement
   b. Power
   c. Sound baffling
   d. Heating and ventilation

e. Lighting
f. Communications equipment (intercoms and telephones)

4. Installing equipment
   a. Delivery schedule
   b. Mode of delivery
   c. Contact upon delivery
   d. Transport to office
   e. Unpacking
   f. Installation and check-out
5. Servicing equipment
   a. Establish service call procedure
   b. Maintain service records (down-time and service response)
   c. Monitor service costs and adjust maintenance contracts accordingly
6. Documenting performance impact and adjusting standards.

Once the schedule is established, follow-through is in order. Since many items are interrelated, it's important to comprehend the total impact of schedule changes. Frequent checks with the vendors and internal service organizations involved are necessary in order to stay abreast of developments beyond your control. As delivery dates change, schedule adjustments have to be made accordingly. If system delivery is delayed, facilities work may have to be rescheduled and operator training moved to a later date. When operators are trained too early, they tend to forget much of what they learn in class and must struggle to become proficient. The ideal situation is to have equipment waiting at the office when they return from their training class. When the installation is made, it's time to begin a new phase—smoothing out wrinkles and monitoring the impact of the new system.

Follow-through is a vital factor

8-17. Monitor Performance through Models

Let things settle down before your next change

If you've followed the process outlined in this chapter, a business model will exist upon installation of the new equipment. It's a good idea to let things settle down before diving off into the development of a new set of model indices. Once the operators become relatively proficient in using the new system, then you can begin changing model information. This will let you compare actual to projected performance. If your assumptions were correct, you'll probably want to pass your findings along to management.

Indices show bottlenecks

In addition to checking your system expectations, the model will identify problem areas in the new system. Your indices will let you know when process points are out of balance with others. Additional adjustments, modifications, and even the need for additional pieces of equipment may be called for through feedback provided by the system model. Through regular review of a well-developed business model, you can optimize business system performance.

9-1. INTRODUCTION

Now that you have a feel for word processing systems and their use and are familiar with your own business system in terms of performance and functional need, you're ready to start looking at word processing systems. This chapter deals with system selection. It provides tips on

1. How to evaluate systems based on specific business needs
2. How to deal with word processing system sales representatives
3. How to dig out those often unseen "hidden costs."

You're ready to look at WP systems

9-2. WORD PROCESSING SYSTEM EVALUATION

There are a number of important aspects in evaluating word processing systems—or any new asset, for that matter. These include knowing what your operation needs today as well as what it will need in three to five years. It's extremely important to stay

9 Selecting Your System

in touch with the direction of the business in terms of growth, changes in business orientation, and any other organizational modifications that can affect system modifications. Once you understand where the business is going, you're ready to begin seeing what can be done to improve operational efficiencies. This section approaches the evaluation process systematically. The first steps are

Know the business direction

1. Developing a weighted needs list
2. Developing a system comparison matrix.

9-3. Developing a Weighted Needs List

Define what's important

Before setting out on your quest for the right or best system for your specific applications, it's a good idea first to take stock of what features are most important to you. Some features may be extremely important to increased productivity, while others will only be used on an occasional basis. A few may be completely useless. This is where weighting comes in. The first step is to make a list of every word processing feature that has any application to the business. Once the list is made, it must be prioritized in accordance with the impact that features can have on business efficiency.

Frequency of use and functional impact

The frequency with which features will be used is important, but the real key is their overall performance benefit to the business. For instance, automatic centering may be used several times each day, while the sort feature may only be used a few times each week. It's entirely possible, however, that the functional value of sort may be much greater to the business than centering. If this is the case, sort would be weighted more heavily than center. So there are two dimensions that influence weighting and thus prioritization of your feature list: frequency and functional value. Let's look at both of these factors and then at a typical example of weighting.

9-4. Weighting by Frequency of Use. When analyzing features in terms of frequency of use, it's necessary to look at the way things are presently done and then determine how they will be done as a system feature. For example, if keyboard operators have to center manually, how often do they do it? By studying a sample period of work, you may find that your operators manually center text information an average of ninety-two times in 264 pages of documentation prepared over an eleven-day period. Of course, the greater the sample, the better the data should be.

How often is it used?

If the 264-page figure is considered a representative sample and each operator produces five hundred pages per month, this means that the operator will average 174 centering transactions each month, or an average of one centering transaction per hour (173.33 hour/work month).

The calculation for frequency weighting is

$$\frac{ST_n}{SU_n} \times \frac{U_n \text{ per mo.}}{173.33 \text{ hr./mo.}} = T_f \text{ per hour}$$

where

ST_n is the number of transactions in a sample (centering operations)

SU_n is the number of sample units (pages of text)

U_n per month is units produced per month per operator (500 pages)

173.33 hr./mo. is the number of hours worked per operator per month

T_f per hour is the transaction frequency per hour.

Using the numbers from the above example,

$$\frac{92}{264} \times \frac{500}{173.33} = 1.005 \text{ transactions per hour}$$

Standardize frequency

Instead of times per hour, you may want to know how many times per month a feature is used. If this be the case, simply disregard dividing by 173.33.

The frequency of use of every important feature can be calculated in the above manner. Once you have determined how many times each feature can be used, you're ready to calculate the functional value of each feature.

9-5. Weighting by Functional Value. Functional value is basically the time saved by a new feature each time it is used. To calculate functional value, the time required to perform a specific business function is compared on a before-and-after basis. For example, if manual alphabetizing of a five-page mailing list takes one hour and forty minutes (or 100 minutes) and automatic sorting with a word processing system takes three minutes and forty-five seconds (or 3.75 minutes), the functional value (or time saved) is 96 minutes and 15 seconds.

Time saved by each use

100 minutes − 3.75 minutes = 96.25 minutes.

Now that the functional value is known, it can be combined with the frequency to obtain the total value.

9-6. Combining Frequency and Functional Value. If the frequency of mailing list sorting is twice each week (or 8.66 times per month), and the functional value is 96.25 minutes, the total value of the feature to the business will be

8.66 times per mo. × 96.25 minutes = 833.525 min. per mo.

This is 13 hours and 53 minutes per month savings (or 4.8 minutes per hour) for this particular feature.

9-7. Assigning Weighted Values. Once all important features have been computed as to their weighted values, the prioritization process can begin. Values should be in consistent terms: savings per month, per week, per day, or per hour. The most valuable features should be assigned the highest numerical values. The least important ones should be assigned the lowest numerical values. A numerical value system, such as ranking from 1 to 10 in importance, can be used to keep comparison computations simple. Whatever system you decide upon, it's *relative value* that's important. This is vital in comparing your specific business needs to solutions offered by word processing systems. With the weighted values in hand, you're ready to begin the next step in system analysis, developing a system comparison matrix.

Weighted value based on benefit

9-8. Developing a System Comparison Matrix

A system comparison matrix is an excellent tool for evaluating competing word processing systems. The comparison matrix, which can be several pages in length, provides an objective checklist of system features, pricing, manufacturer information, and other characteristics that are important to system selection. These system characteristics are listed vertically at the left edge of each page of the matrix. The systems being compared are located horizontally across the top of each page. In this way, characteristic evaluation comments can be entered in the matrix and then compared directly for each system. Tables 9-1 and 9-2 are sample comparison matrices. In Table 9-1, specific weighted values, answers such as "yes," "no," "good," "fair," or "poor" (G/F/P), or specific numerical values can be entered. Table 9-2 varies from Table 9-1 in that it simply compares features between three photocomposition systems being evaluated. It doesn't use weighted values, nor is it as thorough an analysis as Table 9-1.

An objective checklist

Comparing systems to weighted value and to each other

Table 9-1. Sample Word Processing System Comparison Matrix

Description	Weighted Value	System A	System B	System C	System D	System E
Monthly Lease:						
Work station						
Printer						
CPU						
Storage device						
Forms tractor						
Sheet feeder						
Cabinets						
Work tables						
Cables						
Adapters						
Special software						
Sort						
Data entry						
Mathpak						
Telecommunication						
List/Merge						
Other (specify)						
________________						
________________						
Purchase Price:						
Work station						
Printer						
CPU						
Storage device						
Forms tractor						
Sheet feeder						
Cabinets						

Table 9-1 (continued)

Description	Weighted Value	System A	System B	System C	System D	System E
Work tables						
Cables						
Adapters						
Special software						
Sort						
Data entry						
Mathpak						
Telecommunication						
List/Merge						
Other (specify)						
______________________						
______________________						
Purchase discount						
Service:						
Service distance (mi.)						
Quoted response time						
Service charges						
Lease						
Purchase						
Training:						
Number of trainees at no charge						
Training charge/operator						
Training location						
Publications:						
Operating instructions						
Quick-reference cards						
Training manuals						

Table 9-1 (continued)

Description	Weighted Value	System A	System B	System C	System D	System E
Supply catalog						
Other (describe)						
______________________						
Supplies:						
Local source						
Delivery time						
Font charge						
Ribbon charge						
Storage media charge						
Other (specify)						
______________________						
______________________						
System Type:						
Stand-alone						
Shared-logic						
Distributed-logic						
Timeshared						
System Configuration:						
Display						
Nondisplay						
Minimum work stations						
Maximum work stations						
Max. WS distance from CPU						
Working Storage Media:						
Single diskette						
Dual diskette						
Tape cassette						

Table 9-1 (continued)

Description	Weighted Value	System A	System B	System C	System D	System E
Dual tape cassette						
Hard disk						
Other (specify)						
______________________________						
Memory size (std. text pp.)						
Archive Storage Media:						
Reel tape						
Hard disk						
Diskette						
Other (specify)						
______________________________						
Keyboard:						
Detached						
Total keys						
No. of function keys						
No. of cursor-control keys						
Display Type:						
CRT						
Plasma						
LED						
LCD						
Other (specify)						
______________________________						
No. characters/screenload						
Number of lines						
No. of strip display characters						
Without display						

Table 9-1 (continued)

Description	Weighted Value	System A	System B	System C	System D	System E
Display Control:						
Horizontal scroll						
No. of characters						
Vertical scroll						
Split screen						
Full-page zoom						
Cursor intensity (G/F/P)						
Brightness control						
Contrast control						
Displayed character size						
Screen graphics						
Greek						
Math						
Special (specify)						
______________________________						
Right justify						
Sub/superscript						
Format display (G/F/P)						
Information display						
Document name						
Document ID no.						
Page position						
Line position						
Character position						
Margin settings						
Spacing						
Tab settings						
Operator prompts						

Table 9-1 (continued)

Description	Weighted Value	System A	System B	System C	System D	System E
Character highlighting						
During insert						
During delete						
During move						
During copy						
Other (specify)						
______________________						
Reverse color						
Reflection control						
Automatic System Features:						
Number of function keys						
Number of mnemonics						
Strikeover						
Destructive space						
Insert						
Delete						
Move						
Within document						
Other document						
Other storage medium						
Text adjust						
Copy or duplicate						
Within document						
Other document						
Other storage medium						
Text adjust						
Underscore						
Deunderscore						

Table 9-1 (continued)

Description	Weighted Value	System A	System B	System C	System D	System E
Underscore on screen						
Double underscore						
Abort function						
Center between margins						
Center over column						
Standard tab						
Decimal or align tab						
Hyphenation						
Dehyphenation						
Search						
Replace						
Global replace						
Line return						
Global pagination						
Global depagination						
Reformat						
No. formats/p.						
Auto. line return						
Auto. word wrap						
Auto-advance keys						
Spacebar						
N,S,E,W keys						
Backspace						
Blank						
Period						
Hyphen						
Underscore						
Other						

Table 9-1 (continued)

Description	Weighted Value	System A	System B	System C	System D	System E
Right justification						
Displayed						
Column move						
Column switch						
Column insert						
Column delete						
Column replace						
Document assembly						
List/Merge						
Glossary or user defined keys						
No. of characters						
Complexity (G/F/P)						
Automatic headers						
Automatic footers						
Automatic index						
Automatic front matter						
Table of contents						
List of illus.						
List of tables						
Automatic work measurement						
File index (G/F/P)						
File index search by						
Document name						
Document no.						
Author name						
Operator name						
Date filed						

Table 9-1 (continued)

Description	Weighted Value	System A	System B	System C	System D	System E
Sort						
Alphabetic						
Numeric						
Alphanumeric						
Ascending						
Descending						
No. of columns						
File size						
Other (specify)						
______________________						
Go to page						
Go to line						
Return to point						
Spelling dictionary						
Lowercase to uppercase						
Uppercase to lowercase						
Prompts						
Informative						
Action						
Evaluation (G/F/P)						
Menus						
Main menu						
Print menu						
File index menu						
Telecomm. menu						
Sort menu						
Math menu						

Table 9-1 (continued)

Description	Weighted Value	System A	System B	System C	System D	System E
Other System Features:						
Concurrent input-output						
Forms tractor						
Sheet feeder						
Envelope handling						
Concurrent operator activity						
System response (G/F/P)						
Dual-column printout						
Single document						
Two document						
All margins justified						
Appears on screen						
Two-column edit on screen						
Printer Type:						
Selectric						
Daisy						
Thimble						
Keybar						
Ink Jet						
Thermal						
Laser						
Line						
Other (specify)						
______________________________						
Single or double head						
Printer Control:						
Line spacing						

Table 9-1 (continued)

Description	Weighted Value	System A	System B	System C	System D	System E
Single						
1½						
Double						
2½						
Triple						
Variable						
Superscript/Subscript						
Pitch						
8						
10						
12						
15						
Proportional						
Unrestricted						
Strike control						
Single only						
Double						
Triple						
Bold or shadow print						
Print Wheel						
Metal						
Plastic						
No. of fonts available						
Special character fonts (specify)						
______________________						
______________________						
Incremental spacing control						
Printer speed						

Table 9-1 (continued)

Description	Weighted Value	System A	System B	System C	System D	System E
40 cps						
55 cps						
120 cps						
200 cps						
400 cps						
Other (specify)						
______________________						
Impact control						
Platen width						
Ribbon widths						
1/4 inch						
5/16 inch						
Mathematics package						
Add						
Subtract						
Multiply						
Divide						
Symbols in text						
Crossfoot						
Ease of programming (G/F/P)						
No. of equations per operation						
No. of computations per document						
Programing Capability:						
Assembly language						
BASIC						
COBOL						
FORTRAN						

Table 9-1 (continued)

Description	Weighted Value	System A	System B	System C	System D	System E
PASCAL						
RPG						
Other (specify)						
________________						
Telecommunication Features:						
Baud rate(s)						
Word length						
Parity						
Stop bits						
Protocol						
ASCII						
EBCDIC						
2741						
Other						
________________						
Autodial						
Autoanswer						
Foreground						
Background						
Interactive						
Batch						
Productivity Statistics:						
Keystrokes per document						
Time per document						
Data by operator						
Date and time processed						

Table 9-1 (continued)

Description	Weighted Value	System A	System B	System C	System D	System E
Pages printed						
Lines printed						
Other (specify)						

Table 9-2. Photocomposition Comparison Matrix

Feature	System A	System B	System C
Monthly rental	$825/mo.	$1,875/mo.	$855/mo.
Upgradability	$150/mo./terminal	$350/mo./terminal	$395/mo./terminal
Technology	software-based	hardware-based	software-based
WP front end	yes	no	disk compatibility
WP interface	hard-wired	disk conversion	disk compatibility
Concurrent input-output	yes	yes (if I/O same format)	yes
File management	excellent	directory of 1st 16 char. of each job	26-line list of 1st 64 char. of each job
Speed	50 11-pica lpm	50 11-pica lpm	50 11-pica lpm
Line length	48 pica (8 in.)	45 pica (8 in.)	45 pica (70 pica option)
Paper width	8 inches	8 inches	8 inches (12 inch option)
Resident type styles	8 (4 segments × 2 faces)	8 (2 segments × 4 faces)	16 (4 segments × 4 faces)
Type sizes	19 (from 6 to 54 point)	16 (from 5½ to 72 point)	70 (from 5½ to 74 point)
Maximum document size	20 feet long	6,000 char.	8,000 char.
Screenload	24 lines × 80 char.	15 lines × 80 char.	13 lines × 80 char.

Table 9-2 (continued)

Feature	System A	System B	System C
Reverse leading	15 inches	1 inch standard (12 inch option)	16 inches
Greek and math display	limited (uses look-up table)	no	yes
Horizontal scroll	yes	no, wraps lines	no, wraps lines
Line endings displayed	yes	yes	yes
Productivity statistics	yes	no	limited
Telecommunications	yes	yes	yes
Global search/replace	yes	no	yes
Boilerplate glossary	yes	no	yes
Hyphenation dictionary	15,000-word programable	rules of English algorithm	rules of Engl. & 10,000-char. programable
Format storage	250 areas up to 15,000 char.	16 burst keys @ 256 char./key	99 areas up to 2,000 char.
Training	in-house, no chg.	in-house, $300 for follow-up	in-house, no. chg. for follow-up
Service	rated fair	rated poor	rated excellent
Publications	good	fair	good

9-9. HOW TO DEAL WITH WORD PROCESSING SALES REPRESENTATIVES

Sales personality versus sales value

Salespeople play a key role in the decision-making process. Often choices are based on the best salesperson instead of the best product value. The smoothest-talking, best-looking salesperson with the fattest expense account for lunch and cocktails is often the most successful. Be wary and, above all, be sure to select equipment based on its merit. After all, the equipment will be around a lot longer than the salespeople.

Objectivity plays a vital role in the selection process. This section presents a few suggestions on how to deal with a word processing system sales representative. Included is information on

1. Getting the sales representative's attention
2. Getting the most out of a product demonstration
3. Avoiding the sales of "futures."

Some important steps

9-10. Getting the Sales Representative's Attention

If your company is large and well known, most salespeople will be anxious to come talk to you. However, if yours is a small, relatively unknown company, you may find that the salespeople have "bigger fish to fry." They like their customers to be "qualified," that is, each must be a bonafide prospect. If there's any doubt, they may put you off.

9-11. Let Them Know You're Serious. It's imperative, especially if you're a small outfit, to impress upon the sales representative that you are seriously interested in buying a word processing system. If you let the salesperson know you're in the decision-making process, he or she will be more eager to talk to you. Your urgency becomes the rep's urgency. Also, knowing that you can discuss systems intelligently lets the representative know you've been researching the subject and have some idea as to what you're getting into.

Appear ready

9-12. Make the Most of Your First Visit. Once you have the sales representative's attention, make an appointment. The normal procedure is for him or her to drop by your office for discussion and, while there, to invite you to his or her office for a system demonstration. If you are asked to go to another customer's operation for a demonstration, you'd better check out the sales representative: a lack of office space and

Are they committed?

equipment to demonstrate sometimes indicates a lack of commitment. It can be a waste of your time and the sales representative's to come by your office if you believe you already have an idea of what's needed.

Of course, salespeople often feel they can be more helpful by seeing your operation and the problems you're trying to solve. However, if you already understand the problems and know what solutions you're looking for, it will be more efficient for you to go directly to the sales representative's office. You can discuss the details, see the equipment, take a look at the size of the organization that will be responsible for system support, obtain all available product literature, and get a demonstration in one session.

9-13. Getting the Most out of a Product Demonstration

The product demonstration is an important event, and as such it should be fully exploited. Six things are recommended:

Six recommendations

1. Schedule ample time—a minimum of two hours.
2. Ensure that an experienced operator conducts the demonstration.
3. Actively participate in the demonstration.
4. Bring along one or two of your senior operators.
5. Fill out your checklist.
6. Get a list of current users.

9-14. Schedule Ample Time. It's impossible to really see what a state-of-the-art word processing system can do in a brief session. If you get a thirty-minute demonstration and a two-hour lunch, you've wasted your time. Let the sales representative know you're really interested. The time you spend will be key to your decision. Early morning or after lunch is usually the best time for a demonstration. When the sales representative knows you want to spend enough time to get a good look, they will be better prepared for a thorough demonstration.

Don't waste your time

9-15. Ensure That an Experienced Operator Conducts the Demonstration. If you want to see what a word processing system can do, ensure that an experienced operator is present to put the machine through its paces. Salespeople are often quite familiar with the system, but sometimes they are not good operators. In fact, there are some who barely type. If you want to ring the system out and get real-world answers about specific features and key sequences, be sure there's an experienced operator present. Many demonstrations are a waste of time and a disservice to the system when no one is available to show it properly.

Prepare to see all

9-16. Actively Participate in the Demonstration. To get the most out of the demonstration, take an active role in it. Often, a "canned" demonstration is put together to demonstrate as many features as possible in the shortest amount of time. Take notes during the canned segment; once it is over, go back over your notes and ask questions that may not have been answered. Sit down at the keyboard yourself and go through a few simple operations such as strikeover, delete, insert, and move. There's no better substitute for understanding how the system works than actually putting it through its paces yourself. You'll get direct feedback as to its functionality and ease of use.

Try it yourself

Another way to participate in the demonstration is to bring actual samples of work to be done or forms to be used on the system. This lets you see exactly what the system benefits and limitations are when applied to real office problems.

9-17. Bring Along One or Two of Your Senior Operators. It can be quite beneficial to bring one or two of your senior operators to a demonstration. First, they tend to ask very good questions. The questions are usually on a detailed level and often uncover what might seem minor points that can really be major barriers if left unasked. A second and equally important benefit is that by having your operators assist in the system analysis process, the ultimate decision will be partially theirs. This makes them more committed to successful system implementation, and helps to sell other operators within the organization.

Several advantages

9-18. Fill Out Your Checklist. The last thing you should do after seeing the demonstration is fill out your system comparison matrix (checklist). Let the sales representative and the operator respond to your questions. Don't tell them they're being compared; simply let them know you're seeing what the system will do in your particular application. Skip over the obvious answers and concentrate on those that you need help with. Once done, you'll have an excellent system evaluation that will serve you well when it's time to determine which system best fits your operation.

Get all the answers

9-19. Get a List of Current Users. An important service your sales representative can perform is providing you with a list of current system users. If there is a reluctance to do this, be careful. After all, if the system is as good as the sales representative would have you believe, he or she should be delighted to let you check with present users. The list of system users lets you verify both system performance in an operational environment and customer satisfaction. You can check on service, training, equipment reliability, and functionality, and you will likely discover some system applications you never thought of. Proper use of the list of system customers can be the most valuable input you receive when considering a certain word processing system.

Check with other customers

9-20. Avoiding the Sale of Futures

The term *futures* refers to features that are promised or expected to be added to a word processing system at some date in the future. There's not a system salesperson in the world who doesn't have a "wish list" for his or her system. There are always things the salesperson would like to have that would give his or her system an edge and make it easier to sell. All representatives sincerely want their system to be all things to all people.

Don't buy wishes

Frequently, system manufacturers do have a number of new features on the drawing board, in development, or in test. Whenever salespeople get wind of a new feature, you can bet they'll let you know that they're coming out with it (even if they're not supposed to tell you). Then there are features not presently offered by their system that are referred to as "not out yet." This is an expression frequently used even when a feature hasn't been thought about by the manufacturer.

This can be misleading to an inexperienced word processing system analyst, particularly when a time frame like "sometime next year" is mentioned. Even if you get a date, don't write it down. There's just too much at stake. New features may actually be in the works, but the technology involved often makes the installation of these features unreleasable. Adding one feature sometimes affects the efficiency of others, and the system can wind up in terminal crash. The moral of this discussion is, Don't believe it until you see it. Consider only those features that you can see demonstrated. Don't buy futures.

If you don't see it, don't count on it

9-21. HOW TO DIG OUT THOSE HIDDEN COSTS

There are a number of expenses associated with operating a new piece of high-technology equipment. This section describes a number of these to help you get to the final price tag of installing a word processing system. The costs come in several categories. These include

Look at all the costs

1. Capital expense
2. Freight expenses
3. Facilities expense
4. Installation expense
5. Occupancy
6. Supply expense
7. Peripheral equipment expense
8. Training
9. System maintenance
10. Lost time.

9-22. Capital Expense

Capital expense is the purchase price of the equipment being bought. The interest earned on the capital investment is revenue lost to the company. This is offset by tax credits and depreciation. Your accounting department will be able to advise you on the actual impact on cash flow, calculate tax credits, and assign a capital depreciation schedule. To be a good investment, most companies believe that the asset should pay back in something under two years.

If the equipment is acquired on a monthly rental, the expense can be written off in present accounting periods. By renting, you may not accrue equity in the system; if you keep it for a number of years, the cost to your business can become much higher than if you purchased the system. There are some advantages to rental, however:

Rental advantages

1. You have an opportunity to try the system and evaluate vendor service before making a long-term commitment.

2. If better systems come along, you can terminate system rental and order a more efficient system.
3. System maintenance is often provided at no charge.

9-23. Freight Expense

Freight expense is most often FOB point of origin, which is normally the manufacturer's location. In some cases, freight charges are FOB destination, which means that they are "free" to the customer (buried in the price of the equipment). Some vendors will negotiate freight expense; others are firm. In addition to freight expense, you may have to hire a moving crew to transport the equipment from the shipping dock to your office space. However, if you're like most resourceful managers, you'll find a way to get the equipment into your office without using a hired crew. The people in your office are often eager to get the system in place so they can examine it and start using it. An almost festive mood frequently accompanies the receipt of new equipment and mysterious, unopened boxes.

You'll pay one way or another

9-24. Facilities Expense

Facilities work is often considered a capital expense if classified as a building improvement. Regardless of how you classify this cost, it is often quite high. This is particularly true when it requires major rearrangement and utility work. Facilities work can include

1. Electrical power installation
2. Lighting
3. Plumbing (in the case of photocomposer developing equipment)
4. Wall or partition construction

Typical facilities costs

5. Carpeting
6. Cable routing.

Most systems require a computer-grade or "isolated" power source. This prevents voltage transients from surging through the system's power supply from affecting the system's sensitive data-handling circuits. Power sources that are connected to heavy equipment such as copiers or motors can create line noise sufficient to cause system failure. When this happens, data can be lost, and this can be costly to the business. Facilities costs can be a major portion of equipment acquisition dollars and should be reviewed carefully with a qualified architect or facilities engineer.

9-25. Installation Expense

Different manufacturers handle installation charges in different ways. Some install the equipment at no additional cost; some use a flat installation rate. Others quote installation as a percentage of the system's purchase price. Whatever method is used, be sure the vendor explains installation charges, how long it will take to install the equipment after delivery, and when rental charges begin and how they are computed, or, if purchased, when the equipment warranty schedule begins. Purchased equipment normally carries a warranty. This can range from thirty days to twelve months, depending on the vendor. The warranty usually runs from the date of installation. It's a good idea to record the installation date to avoid charges for maintenance that should be performed at no cost.

Check out installation costs up front

9-26. Occupancy

Occupancy is a term used for the space charges incurred by a business. Many businesses apply space charges by the square foot. Regardless of the method used, the impact that a word processing system has

Space is money

on space should be computed. If it requires expansion, and if that expansion adds to the cost of the business, it should be included as part of the cost of system operation.

9-27. Supply Expense

The expense of system supplies is often hundreds and even thousands of dollars per month. Supply utilization should be calculated to determine financial impact. The cost of storage media, printer ribbons, paper, air filters, print fonts, and other incidentals should be calculated as part of the system cost.

Check supplies carefully

9-28. Peripheral Equipment Expense

Peripheral equipment, such as tables, racks for mounting system components, acoustic covers (used to reduce printer noise), cables, and connectors adds up rapidly. When overlooked, two things can happen. First, you may find that the equipment is virtually nonfunctional without some small piece of peripheral equipment. Delay due to lack of this item can be costly as well as embarrassing. Second, the cost of your system will be understated by the amount of the unidentified pieces of equipment, which are sometimes overlooked until the last minute.

Count all the pieces

9-29. Training

Training is often offered at no charge. However, some vendors require that their training operations be self-supporting. When this is the case, there is a training charge for each operator. Whatever the method, the vendor should identify this expense to you before you enter the order. The method of training should also be explained. Some vendors train operators at your place of business, while others train in a classroom.

Training has more than one cost

Training has another cost that is often overlooked. This is the time lost when operators are in training and during the time it takes them to become proficient. Here, the simplicity of the system and the quality of the training pay off. It's always good to determine the standard training time, learning-curve time, and training charges before making an acquisition decision.

9-30. System Maintenance

When a system is leased, maintenance is most often performed at no charge. System maintenance can be arranged in a number of ways. When it is purchased and out of warranty, manufacturers charge for maintenance. Maintenance can be obtained on a call basis; that is, if a system failure is experienced, you'll have to call the manufacturer's maintenance organization and request service. The manufacturer will charge for parts and labor.

Maintenance cost requires analysis

A maintenance contract can be obtained from most word processing system manufacturers. The contract, which normally covers one year's service, covers labor. In some cases certain parts are also covered by the maintenance contract. Many manufacturers increase the price of their maintenance contract if a system is used on more than one shift.

An alternative to vendor maintenance

Some companies, particularly those with large computer installations, employ a staff of maintenance technicians. If this is the case in your company, you may want to send a few technicians to a manufacturer's maintenance school so your equipment can be cared for by in-house personnel. This can be a good approach where well-equipped, competent maintenance people are on the company's payroll. However, the cost for training and equipping technicians can be quite high. In addition to paying for the training course and the technicians' time, spare parts and special tools are often required. Another problem is the potential for turnover. If you make a large investment in training and equipping a technician and he or she leaves the company, you'll have to go through the process again. In the meantime, you'll lose your in-house system coverage.

It's sometimes possible to place problematic system components, such as printers, on maintenance contracts; the more trouble-free components can be serviced on an on-call basis. Where large systems are used, it's often more economical to use on-call service. The alternative may be the purchase of an extremely large maintenance contract costing many thousands of dollars. Whatever you decide, all the costs associated with system maintenance should be computed and included in the total system cost.

Structuring maintenance for economy

9-31. Lost Time

Whenever a new system is installed in a going business, time will be lost. Lost time can be the result of many things, including

1. Training time
2. Learning time (due to operator unfamiliarity with new processes)
3. Equipment downtime (time the equipment is inoperative).

Training time can be computed. Normally, a certain amount of time is allotted for training each operator. Learning time is normally less identifiable. Most managers use trending, or "experience curves." For example, a manager may determine that it will take an operator six weeks to learn a system fully. The operator may be fifty percent proficient during the first week, eighty percent the second, and then gain additional five percent increments in efficiency over the following four weeks. Whatever the formula, learning time is a real cost that should be counted.

Learning time a real cost

Another cost that should be comprehended is equipment downtime. This is a cost that is directly associated with the operational reliability of a system and the quality of service. When reviewing systems, it's always a good idea to get a list of system users to check on reliability and service. If the system is "rock solid," it may be the one for you. If a consensus of users tells you that a particular system is out of service a high percentage of the time due to equipment malfunctions, you'll want to avoid that system. Even when a system is relatively reliable, you'll want to get a report on the responsiveness of the service organization. If it takes several days for a service representative to respond to a service call, you should probably remove that manufacturer from your list of candidates.

Downtime can be expensive

9-32. THE COST-OF-OWNERSHIP APPROACH

The *cost of ownership* includes all costs associated with owning, installing, supplying, operating, and maintaining a piece of equipment. The purchase price of a word processing system is only a portion of the cost of ownership. In this chapter we've looked at a number of costs associated with system ownership. Overlooking any of these costs can result in a distorted view of what the system is contributing financially to the business. By understating the cost of ownership, big dollar amounts can be overlooked and lost. This is one reason that all costs must be identified and added to the bottom line, thereby reducing the potential for financial "gotchas."

The price is only part of the cost

In addition to not knowing all costs associated with system acquisition, you won't have a fair comparison between competing systems. Knowing every system's cost of ownership takes a lot of smoke out of the equation when making system comparisons. For example, a small system selling for $9,000 may not be as financially attractive as one selling for $15,000 because of transportation, installation, maintenance, and supply costs.

Every cost is needed for system selection

In summary, once all costs associated with system ownership are identified, you'll be in a much better position to evaluate the true financial impact that a system has on your business operation, and you'll know which system is truly the best buy.

10-1. INTRODUCTION

This chapter provides some suggestions on how to convince top management, or perhaps convince yourself, that the company's investment in modern office automation equipment is worthwhile. Included in the chapter is discussion on

The investment must be worthwhile

1. The resistance to office automation
2. The use of payback analyses
3. The preparation process
4. The presentation process

10-2. THE RESISTANCE TO OFFICE AUTOMATION

A major barrier to capital expenditures in the office has been management's view of the office as an overhead function. Many seem to think of their office operation as "a necessary evil." The overhead functions have very little to do with the manufacture of the business's product. Spending money in the office just makes the overhead rate higher.

Is office equipment simply overhead—a "business evil"?

10 Selling the Solution

10-3. Reasons for Resistance

There has been an almost natural resistance to office automation on the part of decision makers, and facts seem to bear this out. According to one source, less than three percent of the nation's ten million business sites had installed word processing equipment by the end of the 1970s. At the same time, the capital investment per manufacturing worker had reached $25,000, while capital investment per office worker was at $2,000. (See Figure 10-1.) As a result, factory worker output per labor hour between 1968 and 1978 rose eighty-four percent; office worker output over the same time period rose four percent. This phenomenon is shown in Figure 10-2.

Factory investment much greater than office investment

While relative office productivity is lagging dramatically, office workers' salary increases are averaging seven percent per year in constant dollars, according to Arthur D. Little, Inc., an international consulting firm. According to Booz-Allen and Hamilton, Inc., another international management consulting firm, the total cost of all domestic business office operations was $800 billion in 1979. Of that, $200 billion was spent on space, buildings, computers, telecom-

Overhead costs are rising due to office inefficiencies

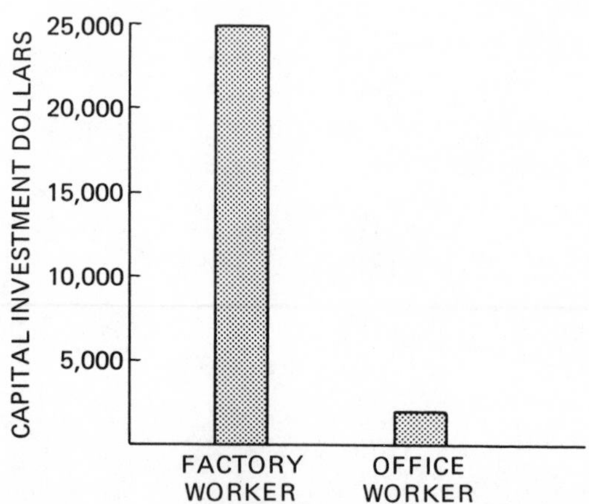

Figure 10-1. Comparing Capital Investment for Factory and Office Workers

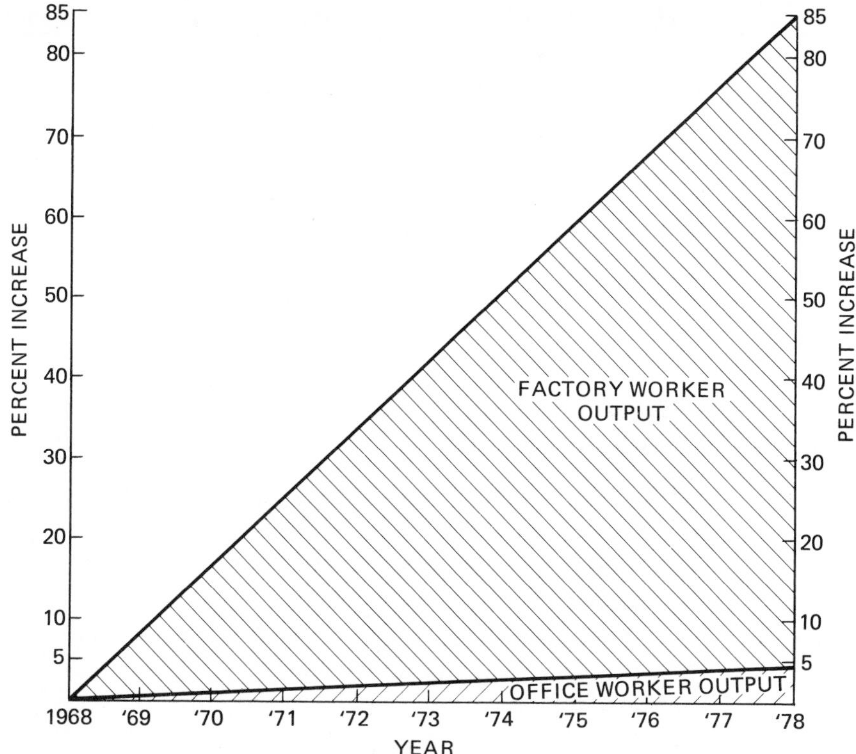

Figure 10-2. Comparing Percent Productivity Increase between Factory and Office Workers over a Ten-Year Period

munications networks, and support services. A staggering $600 billion was spent on labor. The result of all of this is that overhead functions and corresponding overhead rates are becoming more costly as a percent of product cost.

10-4. Managing a Critical Business Resource: Information

The business function performed by office workers is primarily information processing. For businessmen to be convinced of the need for increased automation in the office, they must begin to view information as a critical resource to the success of their business operations. Information can be managed more efficiently through automation. Automation lets fewer people do more, faster, in the same way that automation in a manufacturing operation increases productivity and reduces costs. In fact, office automation should be approached in exactly the same way as manufacturing automation. But convincing top management that there is a real dollars-and-cents payback is the critical issue. If you can't show them savings, you'll never get their support.

Automation in the office makes information processing more cost-effective

10-5. A Positive Outlook toward Office Automation

While there is still heavy resistance to office automation expenditures in many places, there appears to be a general shift in attitudes. Capital expenditures in support of office productivity is on the rise. The New York market research firm, Frost and Sullivan, Inc., predicts that the word processing and office automation market will exceed $300 billion annually through 1987. The dominant hardware includes keyboards, displays, electronic storage devices, and printers.

Office capital on the rise

Word processing equipment has always been predominantly a lease-based business. For one thing, the technology was changing so rapidly that system customers were afraid to purchase something for fear of being left with obsolete equipment. However, the lease trend has been changing. The technology is settling down, and purchases are on the increase. Another reason that purchases are becoming more popular is that an excellent used-equipment market exists. If you decide to buy a new system to replace your old one, there's a good chance you'll find a buyer for the old one with very little difficulty. If you want to test this, just try to find a decent display-based word processor on the used-equipment market. When you do, don't be startled by the price it demands.

Technology stabilization encouraging more office equipment buys

10-6. THE USE OF PAYBACK ANALYSES

Payback analyses, which basically compare system savings to system costs, are essential in determining whether a capital investment has merit or not. Going through the analysis process converts intuition into hard facts that business managers can review, understand, and appreciate. Once you've looked at your present operating costs, as outlined in Chapter 8, and noted what streamlining can save your business operation in terms of labor, material, overhead, supplies, space, quality, and cycle time, you're well along in developing a payback analysis.

Convert intuition into hard facts

10-7. Constructing a Payback Analysis

Once the savings are identified, all the costs of the new system must be added and compared to the savings. Table 10-1 is a sample payback analysis that takes all system costs—that is, both recurring and nonrecurring expenses and capital dollars—and compares them to the savings produced by the system.

Comparing costs to savings

The payback analysis shown in Table 10-1 describes an operation that produces 3,300 pages of text per month. Of the 3,300 pages, 1,550 are new, 1,750 are revised. The labor savings, which includes overhead, is an aggregate figure showing the net savings for all system features. A great deal of leverage is gained through reworking of the 1,750 revised pages which, prior to installation of an automated word processing system, had to be done manually. The automatic word processing system requires only a few keystrokes to modify documents for different applications. The printer plays out these documents automatically, freeing the system operator to work on another job.

Finding payback leverage

Proofreading, editorial, and author-review savings are gained primarily through confidence that unchanged text areas need not be reread. Automated

Author productivity is an area to consider

Table 10-1. Sample Payback Analysis

Description	Old System	New System	Unit Savings	Hourly Savings	Rate/ Cost*	Total Savings
Labor Analysis:						
Keyboard time/p. (all features)	.33/hr	.13/hr	.2/hr			
3,300 pp./mo.	1,089/hr	429/hr		660/hr	$12.26	$8,092
Printer time/p. (handling)	.0125/hr	.003/hr	.0095/hr			
3,300 pp./mo.	41/hr	10/hr		31/hr	$12.26	380
Proofreading time/p.	.1/hr	.02/hr	.08/hr			
1,550 pp./mo	155/hr	31/hr		124/hr	$10.55	1,308
Filing time/doc.	.08/hr	.02/hr	.06/hr			
66 docs./mo.	5.28/hr	1.32/hr		3.96/hr	$12.26	49
Editing time/p.	.15/hr	.07/hr	.08/hr			
1,550 pp./mo.	232/hr	108/hr		124/hr	$22.08	2,738
Author review time/p.	.15/hr	.07/hr	.08/hr			
1,550 pp./mo.	232/hr	108/hr		124/hr	$34.62	4,293
Total labor savings (or loss) per month				1,067/hr		$16,860
Supplies:						
Storage Diskettes	-0-	20	(20)		$8.25	$(165)
Paper (500 sheet/rm)	16.5/rm	9/rm	7.5/rm		$4.27	32
Ribbons	(no difference)					

Liquid paper (cartons)	1	0	1	$10.00	10
Total supplies savings (or loss) per month					$(123)
Occupancy:					
Office area	2,750/sf	2,800/sf	(50/sf)	$ .91	$ (46)
File space	880/sf	650/sf	230/sf	$ .54	124
Total occupancy savings (or loss) per month					$ 78
System Cost:					
Recurring costs					
Maintenance	480/mo	1,420/mo	(940/mo)		$(940)
Telecommunications	-0-	128/mo	(128/mo)		$(128)
Price $128,000 (monthly depreciation @ 5-year straight line)	280/mo	4,495/mo	(4,215/mo)		$(4,215)
less income from present equip. sale (5-year straight line)	43/mo	-0-	43/mo		$ 43
Total recurring cost savings (or loss) per month					$(4,258)
Nonrecurring costs					
Freight	-0-	860	(860)		$(860)
Installation fee	-0-	1,920	(1,920)		$(1,920)
Facilities work	-0-	4,032	(4,032)		$(4,032)
Training	-0-	N/C	-0-		
Total nonrecurring cost					$(6,812)

(continued)

Table 10-1 (continued)

Description	Old System	New System	Unit Savings	Hourly Savings	Rate/ Cost*	Total Savings
Total nonrecurring cost savings (or loss) per month amortized over 5 years @ 15% interest						$ (239)
Payback summary:						
Monthly system savings						
Total labor savings (or loss) per month				1,067/hr		$16,860
Total supplies savings (or loss) per month						$ (123)
Total occupancy savings (or loss) per month						$ 78
Total recurring cost savings (or loss) per month						$(4,258)
Total nonrecurring cost savings (or loss) per month amortized over 5 years @ 15% interest						$ (239)
Total savings (or loss) per month						$12,079
Break-Even Analysis:						
Purchase price			$128,000			
Make-ready			6,812			
Total			$134,812			

$$\frac{\$\ 134{,}812}{\$\ 12{,}079/\text{mo}} = \text{11.16-month payback}$$

*Labor savings includes overhead.

word processing systems eliminate typographical error "creep-in" from manual rekeyboarding.

There are many other areas that can generate savings that have not been included in the table. For instance, if the operation used outside photocomposition services, it would be charged $20 to $35 per manually typeset page. With the automated system, many vendor services are available that charge $10 to $15 per telecommunicated typeset page. Only two hundred pages per month at $10 per page savings produce $2,000 gross savings.

Vendor services a potential savings

The use of a central dictation system is another area for savings. Time saved by both authors and transcriptionists can be computed here. Other areas for savings include administrative support features such as programing, math, and work measurement. As a knowledgable business manager, you must decide where your savings are and which systems best yield those savings, and work up a detailed payback analysis to determine break-even.

Dictation and administration support are good payback areas

One additional comment about the information in the table is appropriate. The system in the table carries a purchase price tag of $128,000. The amortization is based on a five-year, straight-line schedule to keep computations simple. However, most businesses amortize on an accelerated schedule, such as sum of the year's digits or double declining balance. You should consult your accountant to determine both the allowable depreciation period and the depreciation schedule to be used.

Amortization usually accelerated

10-8. Other System Benefits

The payback analysis described in paragraph 10-7 dealt with measures that are quantified in dollars and cents. There are other system advantages that can also be shown. Table 10-2 shows other word processing system benefits that are attractive, should be

Money isn't the only benefit

Table 10-2. Other System Benefits

Description	Benefit
Administrative support	System programing and mathematical capabilities can be used to streamline administrative activities and reduce repetitive computation time.
Improved cycle time	Documentation cycle time will be decreased dramatically. "Canned" documents can be regenerated within one day. New documents can be produced on a word processing system in half the time it takes on a manual system.
Improved quality	Documents produced by automatic means will have a much lower error rate than those produced manually. Document quality will reduce customer problems (inaccurate part numbers, etc.) and help create a better company image.
Performance records	The system work-measurement feature provides a job performance record for each document produced. Visibility into operator performance is greatly enhanced by this feature.
Reduced turnover	Higher morale and reduced work tensions resulting from multiple document changes is commonly experienced. Job challenge and personal satisfaction are significantly higher in operations using automatic word processing equipment.
Upgradability	System features offering greater productivity and corresponding savings can be added when needed.

communicated, but are sometimes not directly measurable in dollars.

10-9. THE PREPARATION PROCESS

Collect all the facts

The preparation process includes letting your superiors know about your need for and interest in office automation. It also involves the collection of as much pertinent information as possible that will let you describe the system, show pictures and output samples, and present cases of system applications in other companies, including competitors.

10-10. Communicating Your Need

If you happen to be in a position where you make capital-appropriation decisions, then you won't have to worry about getting people ready to hear your presentation. On the other hand, if you work for a large company that requires capital forecasts for large acquisitions, it's a good idea to start forecasting your system as early as possible.

Forecast as early as possible

Begin by talking to your boss about word processing systems so that he or she will be familiar with your project when the time comes to show your numbers. If at all possible, take him or her along with you on some of your system reviews. You'll find there's nothing more impressive to someone who hasn't seen a word processing system in action than a live demonstration.

Let the boss see first-hand

Of course, each manager-subordinate relationship is different. You'll have to be the judge of how to approach your boss when trying to gain backing for the system. The main thing is "no surprises." Keep the boss apprised of your interest and analysis work. When the final presentation time approaches, the boss will not only be ready, he or she will be eager to see the numbers.

"No surprises" the best policy

10-11. Collecting Pertinent Information

Another important part of the preparation process is the collection of pertinent information that will help make a favorable impression on those responsible for approving the acquisition of the word processing system. Foremost is the collection of financial facts. This makes the decision easy for business managers responsible for maximizing profitability.

Make the decision easy

Next, be sure to have good descriptive information available. If the reviewing managers understand what

A picture is worth a thousand words

the system looks like and does, they'll feel much more comfortable about an approval decision. Have equipment brochures, pictures, and, if possible, samples of work produced on the system.

Show where others in your industry are

Another important resource in support of your case is information about other companies in your industry that are successfully using word processing systems. Your sales representative will usually give you a list of his customers with names and phone numbers of the responsible people. By making a few phone calls, you can provide details about system applications and performance improvements being experienced. When appropriate, it's sometimes good to point out direct competitors who are using systems advantageously. If their system is putting them in a favorable cost situation, your management may feel it is mandatory to improve business performance through office automation.

10-12. THE PRESENTATION PROCESS

A strategy is a must

Once you have done all the analysis work, forecast the project through the company's financial channels, communicated your intentions to your boss, and pulled together equipment description material and case studies, you're ready to begin the presentation process. This process has two general components: strategy and delivery. The next two paragraphs describe these components.

10-13. The Presentation Strategy

Every company has its presentation structure. Most large companies have a capital review panel made up of high-level managers. These managers often work with a fixed capital budget. They meet monthly or quarterly, listen to presentations, rank capital projects in accordance with company need, and approve requests based on capital funding availability. Whatever the format, it's important to ensure that you have a strategy for your presentation.

10-14. Presentation Timing. The best time to request capital funds is when the business outlook is good and funding is available. You might have the most convincing presentation in the world, but if the economy is in a downturn or if there's a major disaster in the factory that requires heavy funding to fix, project approval will be tough. Check with the accounting people. They can normally tell you what your probability is. You also might have a friend or two who sits on the capital review panel. It won't hurt to discuss your project with them to see if there are any conflicting problems. When the time is right, be sure you're in there pitching. If it's bad, wait for things to improve.

Choose the right time

10-15. Know What to Expect. The formats of capital review meetings vary. A few are stiff and formal. Some use overhead projection foils and special forms. Many simply have presenters pass around information packets and go through the pages discussing details and answering questions. Others are extremely informal. Whatever the format, know what to expect. If you haven't been through a panel review, talk to people who have. Be prepared to present in a way that is acceptable to the reviewers.

Know the ropes

10-16. Package Your Presentation for Efficiency. When going through the structure of your presentation, realize that you will have only a few minutes of the panel's time. Prepare material that says the most in the least space. Be sure that the bottom line is clear. The dollars saved and the payback are the biggest guns you have. Highlight this information so it is crystal clear. If possible, have photographs of the system. It's worthwhile to let the panel see what they're buying.

Make sure the punch line is loud and clear

10-17. Have Back-Up Information Available. It's usually a good idea to be as brief as possible, but have your *back-up* ready. If you are questioned on details, have all the answers on hand. This is particularly true when panel members ask for alternatives. Be ready to show choice number two and even number three if necessary. But be able to defend your first selection in dollars and cents. If they can't afford number one and want you to pursue choice number two, know whether or not it's the right thing to do, and let them know, too. It may be worthwhile to suggest that you return in a month or two in pursuit of the first choice as opposed to settling for a system configuration that will lose the business money in the long term.

Be prepared to discuss the alternatives

10-18. The Presentation Delivery

Once you're prepared, you should be ready to deliver. A professional-quality presentation is imperative. You should make a good personal appearance, have a well-rehearsed address with ready answers to potential questions, and have presentation material of good quality, arranged in the proper order.

A smooth delivery best

10-19. Arrange Your Presentation in the Proper Order. It's advisable to number your slides. If you drop them or they fall off a table, it may take what can seem an eternity to get them back in order. Plan to show only those few pages of material that tell the financial story, describe benefits to the business, and help the panel members to visualize the system. These should be on top of the presentation packet for easy access. Your back-up, which may be extensive, should be indexed so that information can be quickly retrieved in response to a panel member's question. If you fumble around looking for a slide, you may give the impression of not being prepared.

Have your presentation organized and numbered

10-20. Check the Accuracy of Your Data. Your presentation should be as informative as possible, and the integrity of your data should be perfect. Every number should be checked and double-checked. If you show numbers that don't add up, the entire presentation will lose its credibility. Never imply that

Data integrity key to credibility

your project is anything more than an opportunity for the company to make a good business investment.

10-21. Use the Right Tone. Be sure that your presentation is businesslike and confident, but not tutorial. You can lose the support of panel members by using the wrong tone. Some might even take offense to the point of becoming angry. You may find some panel members quite knowledgeable about office automation and word processing systems. Don't be surprised if they ask in-depth questions about system features and make suggestions for additional applications pertaining to their area of expertise.

Don't preach

10-22. SUMMARY

This book started with the premise that you knew very little about word processing systems and ends with the assumption that you are knowledgable enough to analyze, select, and cost-justify a sophisticated word processing system. Indeed, if you read this book, studied your own business operation, reviewed word processing system vendor literature, and attended system demonstrations, you should be as ready as anyone. The major problems in businesses today are

Three major barriers

1. Justifying system costs to superiors
2. Choosing the right system
3. Making productive use of the system once it is installed.

Once the system is in, don't let up

The book should be a helpful tool in items 1 and 2. Point 3, which starts upon system installation, is up to you. If you developed a business model for the cost justification process as described in Chapter 8, point 3 above should be achievable. By keeping a model of the business operation, you can maintain continual feedback relative to system performance. The model will let you identify low-performance areas, take corrective actions, and monitor the results of those actions. But all of this is a matter of business discipline. You can install a system and just let things happen, or you can have the most efficient operation in the world.

Improving the capacity for better decisions

In either case, once you have gone through the process of observing the human relations involved in change, developing an understanding for automated business systems, analyzing their impact on the business performance, comparing them to one another, and cost-justifying their acquisition, you will have lived an extremely interesting and rewarding business experience. Not only will this experience make you more aware of opportunities for greater business efficiencies, but it should also provide a basis for the understanding, analysis, and solution of many other business-related problems; all of this should lead to an improved capacity for making better business decisions.

Index